Latin

100 ESSENTIAL CDs | THE ROUGH GUIDE

There are more than two hundred Rough Guide travel,
phrasebook, and music titles, covering destinations from
Amsterdam to Zimbabwe, languages from Czech to
Vietnamese, and musics from World to Opera and Jazz

Other 100 Essential CD titles

Blues • Classical • Country • Jazz
Opera • Reggae • Rock • Soul • World

www.rou

Rough Guide Credits

Text editors: Orla Duane, James McConnachie
Series editor: Mark Ellingham
Production: Helen Prior, Zoe Nobes

Publishing Information

This first edition published November 2001 by
Rough Guides Ltd, 62–70 Shorts Gardens, London, WC2H 9AH

Distributed by the Penguin Group

Penguin Books Ltd, 80 Strand, London, WC2R 0RL
Penguin Putnam, Inc., 375 Hudson Street, New York 10014, USA
Penguin Books Australia Ltd, 487 Maroondah Highway,
PO Box 257, Ringwood, Victoria 3134, Australia
Penguin Books Canada Ltd, 10 Alcorn Avenue, Toronto,
Ontario, Canada M4V 1E4
Penguin Books (NZ) Ltd, 182–190 Wairau Road,
Auckland 10, New Zealand

Typeset in Bembo & Helvetica to an original design by Henry Iles.
Printed in Spain by Graphy Cems.

A catalogue record for this book is available from the British Library.
ISBN 1-85828-733-2

Latin

100 ESSENTIAL CDs | THE ROUGH GUIDE

by Sue Steward

with reviews by

David Cleary, Jan Fairley, Mary Farquharson, Tommy
Garcia, Chris Moss, Dan Rosenberg
and Phil Sweeney

ROUGH
GUIDES

Contents

Introduction

Twenty years ago, buying salsa, samba, bossa nova or tango records was a challenge anywhere outside Latin America or the *barrios* (Latin neighbourhoods) of the USA. Since then, however, non-Latinos world wide – from New York to London, and from Istanbul to Hong Kong – have discovered the joy that is Latin music, flocking to salsa classes and music shops that stock Latin CDs alongside MTV rock and dance.

No one event could have single-handedly transformed the music's status, but there's no doubting the significance of *Buena Vista Social Club* – the album and the film by Wim Wenders. Astounded to see the tiny World Circuit label selling over five million copies of the album, many major record labels launched a Latin division; BVSC's sensational success coincided with Ricky-mania (salsa purists may sniff, but Ricky Martin is a dedicated propagandist for Puerto Rican traditional music, and he put the island on the map). There were other signs, too: Latin rock singer Gloria Estefan (also featured in this book, though Martin is not) pre-empted BVSC with her late-1980s albums of Cuban and Colombian music, leading many rock fans down the Latin path, and Latin music fans Paul Simon and David Byrne had created their own Latin albums, *Rhythms of the Saints* (Brazilian) and *Rei Momo* (pan-Latin).

So while it is now possible to find a huge range of Latin discs in the shops, a new problem has arisen – what to buy. Faced with racks of albums bearing photos of musicians holding Cuban guitars, Andean flutes, Brazilian drums or Colombian accordions, your instinct might be to choose a compilation or return to more familiar racks – unless you have a friend's recommendation tucked away, or the title of a track you danced to in a club or heard on a specialist radio programme... Which is where 100 Essential Latin CDs – a pocket companion to shopping, real or virtual – comes into its own.

Selecting just 100 albums from the thousands of releases – current, historical, popular, folkloric – created some awful dilemmas and forced some horrible omissions. It was made tolerable (and sometimes even more difficult) by the advice of the specialists who contributed reviews to the book – and who were only too eager to prove just how essential *their* favourites were. The "Further Listening" box at the end of each review is a blessing, a reserve tank for albums by the same artist or by rivals in a related genre, boosting the number of recommended CDs to over 300.

Acknowledgments

For their helpful editorial conversations, and such enthusiastic reviews that I was driven to rush out and buy the things, I would like to thank: David Cleary, Brazil expert, who frequently emailed reviews from "somewhere in the jungle"; Mary Farquharson, former London World Music promoter, now based in Mexico City, who brought Mexican music to life; Tommy Garcia, a true salsa professor and very hard to disagree with on classic salsa; and Dan Rosenberg, nomadic broadcaster on Latin and African music for the global Afro Pop radio station. Edinburgh-based journalist and broadcaster, Jan Fairley, was more than just a contributor, and her advice and encouragement helped gel many editorial decisions – thank you. Thanks also to Chris Moss, in Buenos Aires, and Philip Sweeney, author of the *Rough Guide to Cuban Music*.

Thanks also to London DJs, Gerry Lyseight and John Armstrong; to Simon Broughton, who passed on tips and calmed anxious moments; to David Flower for additional wisdom; and to Orla Duane and James McConnachie, the book´s editors, who did a splendid job. Finally ... thanks to Greg, who uncomplainingly lost a companion for the months it took to produce the book.

Sue Steward

author of *Salsa, Musical Heartbeat of America*, Sue Steward (Thames & Hudson); published in the US as *Musica – Salsa, Rumba, Merengue and More* (Chronicle Books).

Websites

www.descarga.com Hugely well-stocked catalogue of mainly salsa CDs, also offers thumb-nail reviews and invaluable interviews with leading salsa names – living and dead.

www.lamusica.com Fun-packed, magazine-style site from New York, filled with news, reviews and gossipy interviews, plus mail order.

www.amazon.com and **www.amazon.co.uk** Seemingly bottomless well of stock, with occasional short reviews.

Africando All Stars

Mandali

Sterns Africa, 2001

Salif Keita, Koffi Olomide, Thionne Seck, Sekouba Bambino, Ronnie Baro, Gnonnas Pedro, Medoune Diallo, Roger "Shoubou" Eugene, Amadou Balake, Hector Casanova (vocals), and others.

"Africando", in the West-African Wolof language, means "Africa Reunited". It's a title that affirms the musical and historical links between Cuba and the African continent, and an album that yokes together some of Latin music's finest instrumentalists and some of Africa's greatest singers. Malian flautist Boncana Maiga, Africando's musical director, had studied music in Cuba in the 1970s and was heavily influenced by Orquesta Aragón. Later, in New York, he fed his appetite for salsa on releases from the Fania label. In 1991, he approached Senegalese record producer and Cuban music fanatic, Ibrahim Sylla, with a plan to re-work the Cuban classics using a group of African vocalists and New York *salseros* (salsa performers). They rounded up three of their favourite Senegalese singers – Pape Seck, Nicolas Menheim (both ex-Youssou N'Dour band singers) and Medoune Diallo from Orchestre Baobab – and matched them with a back-line drawn from the Fania All Stars and Orquesta Broadway. The resulting album, *Africando – Trovador*, started a tradition that has now reached its fifth release, though Boncana Maiga dropped out and Pape Seck has since died. Each new album widened the musical catchment area, and the musical geography now stretches from New York to Senegal, Mali and the Congo, and back via Cuba, Puerto Rico and Hispaniola.

Mandali opens with Diallo singing the perfectly confected title track – a guttural Wolof croon with a slinky backing of tres guitar and salsa piano. The album's vocal textures are as distinctive as thumb prints, and indeed it is the astonishing vocalists, including "the Golden Voice of Africa", Salif Keita, that make *Mandali* so unique. Keita's re-working of his hit song, **Ntoman**, is outstanding, moulding his declamatory voice to a rocking Cuban groove while enveloped by brass and a lustrous vibraphone. Gnonnas Pedro, a pioneer of such cross-border musical collaborations, takes a sing-song, incantatory approach to **Hwomevonon** with his rough, smoker's voice, and Dakar legend Thionne Seck brings the griot style to **Sey**, creating an effortlessly buoyant and surprisingly gentle tone. Amadou Balake's **Betece** pays tribute to the charanga, with New York Cuban Edy Zervigon (leader of Orquesta Broadway) unleashing a flute solo, while Broadway's one-time singer, Ronnie Baro, slips into a calculatedly over-produced late-1990s salsa groove on **Carpintero**.

From the very different Congolese tradition, Koffi Olomide injects a soulful soukous style to **Mopao**, and Roger "Shoubou" Eugene, leader of Haitian band Tabou Combo, throws another musical genre into the pot with a calypso-salsa version of the Trinidadian classic, "Scandal in the Family", under the title **Scandalo**. Sekouba Bambino, the young Guinean discovery now central to Africando, brings an unrestrained, open-throated griot's flair to **Son Fo**, and also leads the historic vocal get-together which closes the show – the studio microphones were crowded as the soloists and invited chorus took turns to drop verses in Spanish or Wolof onto **Doni Doni**. A long, smooth salsa groove, the track is based on the kind of solo climaxes by the legendary Fania All Stars that had so inspired the African singers in their youth.

Sue Steward

Further listening: Any title by Africando is a delight, but **Vol. 1, Trovador** and **Vol. 2, Tierra Tradicional** (Sterns) are grittier salsa, and feature the stunning, gravelly voice of the late Pape Seck.

José Alberto "El Canario"

Herido (Heartbreak)

Ryko Latino, 1999

José Alberto (vocals, percussion), Alex Mansilla (vocals), Isidro Infante (piano),
Ricky González, Lucho Cueto, Freddy Valdez (piano, keyboards), Francisco Navarro,
Carlos Hayre, Martínez De León (guitar), and others.

"El Canario", José Alberto, is both a New York salsa traditionalist and an experimenter with modern styles. Born in the Dominican Republic in 1958, he moved to Puerto Rico aged seven and from there to New York. He came of age in a city exploding with new salsa, and was quickly drawn into Cuban music. In 1978, he joined the era's influential young charanga band, Típica 73, and cut his teeth singing updated versions of the Cuban classics alongside violin wild-child prodigy Alfredo de la Fé. His nickname, "El Canario" (the Canary), derives from what began as a party trick – he whistles and mimes in uncanny imitation of the trilling concert flutes played in charanga bands, a sound heard here on the bustling **Vete y Pregona**.

El Canario emerged as a distinctive soloist on the historic salsa romantica release of 1982, *Noches Calientes*, and a subsequent string of similarly flavoured albums landed him regularly in the salsa charts. He leads an exhilaratingly rhythmic big band, designed in the late 1980s by RMM label producer Sergio George and carried into the 1990s by Isidro Infante, who co-produced this 1999 release. **Herido** (Heartbreak) also marked the first signing of a major salsa artist to an independent World Music label.

The album opens in typically bouncy and infectious mood

with **Me Dejó Picao**, a showcase for José Alberto's vocal versatility and powers of mimicry – Oscar D'Leon, Gilberto Santa Rosa and Willie Chirino are all evoked. In addition, he reveals a talent for scatting that places him amongst the most inventive jazz singers, a skill displayed in the new Cuban salsa style of **Adonde Vayas**, on which he effortlessly rides the fast, stop-start timba beat and matching bucking horns.

José Alberto's stage performances are slick, precise and hugely enjoyable – he sings, dances and takes solos on timbales, congas and any surface to hand. His reputation as a romantic *salsero* still lingers, no more so than on **La Última Palabra**, a ballad which reveals the distinctive, rich grain of his voice. When he slips into his native rhythm on **Enamorado de Mi País** (In Love With My Country), joined by fellow Dominican, Alex Mansilla, he creates a fast but poised merengue in the style of Mansilla's mentor, Juan Luis Guerra. It possesses all the excitement and crucial ingredients of classic merengue – choppy saxophones, driving, throbbing tambora drum, and a scratchy guiro pulse – but also adds rippling, soukous-style electric guitar riffs and lush, harmonized choruses. Very Guerra. **Déjate Querer** also abandons straight-ahead salsa, this time for a flamenco-influenced, minor-key recounting of a gypsy's plea to a "cruel woman". José Alberto tussles with a barking baritone saxophone, which he calls "*el chivo*" (the goat), while Isidro Infante's distinctive, tinkling piano and a crisp Andalucian guitar weave around the vocal line.

An exquisite Peruvian song, **La Flor de la Canela**, by the legendary singer Chavuca La Grande, brings the album to a surprising close with a tantalizingly brief dialogue between traditional box drum and sweet acoustic guitar.

Sue Steward

Further listening: Típica 73 En Cuba – Intercambio Cultural (Fania) showcases the historic Havana meeting of Cuban pioneers Orquesta Aragón and the young, awed but musically radical New Yorkers. On **Latitudes** (Rykolatino), Cuban violinist Alfredo de la Fé plays the electro-salsa style that he created around his dramatic electric fiddle.

Joe Arroyo

La Noche

World Music Network, 1998

Includes free Colombian sampler CD.

Joe Arroyo (lead vocals), Chelíto de Castro (keyboards), Over López (bass), Alberto Barros (trombone), Armando Galán, Jorge Gaviria (trumpet), Carlos Piña, Libardo Chin, Juventino Ojito, Humberto Ospina (sax, clarinet), Ricardo Ojeda (timbales), Emil Galvis, Neil Benítez (congas), Efraín Villanueva, Ivan Sierra (bongos), and others.

Colombian megastar Joe Arroyo is one of the most effective people-movers in Latin music. His instantly recognizable, high-pitched singing and shrill animal calls, his instinct for an irresistible tune, and his orchestra's sensational sound, have a magnetic appeal to dancers everywhere. In Colombia, he is a household name whose rags-to-riches life story reflects the dreams of his Colombian fans. They have bought his records in millions. In 1990, when he had won the most prestigious Congo de Oro (Golden Congo) award at Barranquilla Carnival several times, a new category, the Super Congo de Oro, was created for him.

Álvaro José Arroyo was born in 1955 near Cartagena. As a young boy he sang in church – and also in the portside cabarets frequented by prostitutes. In 1971, he was taken to Medellín to work with Fruko y los Tesos (Fruko and the Treasures), the flagship youth band of the Discos Fuentes label, producing strings of hits influenced by New York salsa and Cuban son. Their trombone-led hit song, **El Caminante**, reveals Arroyo's voice still young and fresh – smooth, even.

Fruko took his prize young Tesos singers, Arroyo and Wilson

Saoco, into his other band, The Latin Brothers, whose sound was raucous with trombones but sweetened by Chelíto de Acosta's electric piano. The brass-dominated **El Árbol**, and the deviant Cuban son, **El Son Del Caballo**, both recall that heady era. But the best of Arroyo was yet to come: in 1981, he launched his own band, La Verdad, and allowed his voice to follow its natural inclinations. **Las Cajas**, from this period, reveals a consummate vocalist playing with the meanings, rhythms and sounds of words, imitating the instruments and twisting along with their convulsive rhythms. While with La Verdad, Arroyo also showed his skill as a songwriter with a knack for a catchy tune and a universal theme.

This compelling retrospective of Arroyo's songs spans the years spent as a "Teso", as a Latin Brother and with La Verdad. Salsa was Arroyo's original template, but he strayed into other territory, as in his cover of Celina González's hit, **Yo Soy El Punto Cubano**, and in cumbias such as **Suave Bruta**, a sophisticated, loping number, and the catchy **El Gavilán Pollero**, which adds true Colombian flavour. Arroyo continued to break the salsa mould, scooping up rhythms and flavours from around the Caribbean islands – zouk, soca, reggae, Haitian compas – and blending them with Colombian cumbia and Cuban son to create dance forms such as Joe-son, cumbión and son-caribeño. Pure *música tropical*, as the new styles became known.

On the uplifting **La Noche,** a caribeño evoking a night of passion, Arroyo darts around punchy choruses of brass and vocals. **Pal' Bailador** is as straight a son as Arroyo delivers, with meticulously interlocked brass arrangements, but the percussionists still skip to a decidedly Colombian beat. To paraphrase the lyrics of **Mis Zapatos Blancos** – "no white shoes, no dancing" – no Arroyo songs, no salsa party.

Sue Steward

Further listening: Los Tupamaros' **Sufriendo Por Amor** (Vedisco) is another Discos Fuentes album of bright, exhilarating salsa. Like Joe Arroyo, Yuri Buenaventura is a musical magpie who blends salsa and jazzy elements with Afro-Colombian rhythms: try **Herencia Africana** (Caracol).

Susana Baca

Eco de Sombras

Luaka Bop, 2000

Susana Baca (vocals), David Pinto (bass), Rafael Muñoz (guitar), Hugo Bravo (congas, effects, percussion), Juan Medrano Cotito (cajón drum, table, vocals); guests: David Byrne (charango, guitar), Marc Ribot (guitar), Greg Leisz (pedal steel).

Singer, songwriter and folkloricist, Susana Baca grew up in the coastal town of Chorrillos, a suburb of the Peruvian capital, Lima, that was established by the Spanish to house African slave miners – the ancestors of Baca and the present-day Afro-Peruvian community. Baca's father was a fisherman who sang and played guitar, and the sea is a central character in her songs: her music, she says, possesses "the rhythm of the sea".

On stage, she cuts a chic figure, dancing barefoot and swirling her skirts like a Peruvian Isadora Duncan, her body and voice following the subtle rhythms of the cajón, a tuned wooden boxdrum that was originally made by slaves from fruit crates. She sings as casually and intimately as if the massive foreign audiences she meets in Europe or the US were in a local bar at home – and in fact **Eco de Sombras** (Echo of Shadows) was recorded at her home. She is cool and assured, with a pensive air, absorbed in the poetry of her songs.

World Music producer David Byrne heard Baca and her four-piece band during a late-1980s exploratory trip to Peru. He featured her song "Maria Lando" on his compilation, *The Soul of Black Peru*, which also showcased pioneering figures within the Afro-Peruvian tradition, such as poet, guitarist and musicologist, Nicomedes Santa Cruz, and singer Chabuca Grande. Baca and her husband run the Instituto Negrocontinuo in Lima, which rehabilitates endangers Afro-Peruvian music and dance traditions. For *Eco de Sombras*, Byrne introduced Baca to a group of musicians from his New York art-rock set, chosen for their creative openness to Latin music. Together they created a compelling, profound album.

This sensuous collection revolves around Baca's clean, intimate vocal interpretations. As the title implies, the textures resemble shifting shadows and patches of light created by the percussionists and the guitars – electric, acoustic, Hawaiian – and by her magnificent voice, which can switch from teenage lightness to fifty-something maturity. The love songs include thoughtful poems, as in the gorgeous **Poema**, which was originally written by a 1920s Andean poet. In **La Macorina**, by contrast, she revels in blatant eroticism, using tropical fruits as sexual metaphors. The deceptively up-tempo and catchy high-point of the collection is **Valentín**, a powerfully rhythmic piece driven by taut drumming about a sadistic slave driver thrashing a slave – a sound evoked by a cracking whiplash. Byrne and Ribot add spikey electric guitars while Greg Leisz extracts a theramin-like pulse from his pedal steel guitar to build the tension.

Guest percussionist Ciro Baptista boosts Hugo Bravo's regular collection of rhythm sources throughout – an Afro-Brazilian berimbau (squeaky drum) is particularly effective. The stirring Christmas slaves' dance, **Panalivio/Zancudito**, draws on the raw sound of a bowed double bass and African percussion to conjure a conversation between slaves. The contrasting **Xanahari**, an Afro-chant, is backed by a low-key duet between Byrne's charango guitar and an acoustic guitar. In the poignant **Reina Mortal**, Baca sings clipped and crisp to a minimal backing of cajón and slapped double bass, with an acoustic guitar playing soft bossa chords.

Sue Steward

Further listening: Susana Baca (Luaka Bop) is her debut album, while
Afro-Peruvian Classics: The Soul of Black Peru (Luaka Bop) is a beautiful
collection of sung poems and infectious dance tunes.

Ray Barretto

Rican/Struction

Fania, 1979

Ray Barretto (congas), Adalberto Santiago (vocals, percussion), José Fajardo (flute)
Oscar Hernández (piano), Sal Cuevas (bass), Papo Vásquez (trombone), Todd
Anderson (sax), Ralph Irrizary (timbales), Luisito González (bongos), Ray Romero
(batá drum), and others.

Few NuYorican musicians have
had a longer, more varied and
more distinguished career than
conga-player Ray Barretto. Fewer
still have shown such extraordinary persistence and such determination to resist the dilution of
the classic salsa style by new fads
such as disco, hip-hop or even
merengue (although Barretto was
happy to experiment with jazz).
Perhaps only the grievously missed Tito Puente could compare.

Barretto began his career as a teenaged GI in Germany in the
1940s, attempting to emulate the way Chano Pozo had Latinized
Dizzy Gillespie by adding his conga rhythms to a variety of jazz
bands. Then "El Watusi", a comedic boogaloo, gave him a huge
hit which has embarrassed him to this day. Rediscovering his
roots, he formed a Cuban-style violin and flute charanga band,
augmenting it unusually – and wickedly – with trombone, sax
and trumpet. When Barretto first signed to Fania, in 1967, he
switched to the tougher all-horn frontline that would make his
name through the 1970s, with breakthrough hits such as "Acid",
"Indestructible", "Barretto" and, of course, "El Watusi".

Rican/Struction is Barretto's greatest album. It represents a
return to the Fania family of labels and also reconciles Barretto to
his former lead vocalist, Adalberto Santiago, one of five band
members who had wrenched the heart out of his brilliant early

1970s group by leaving to play more "authentic" music with Típica 73. The album confidently attempts to distill the various elements of New York salsa into bravura instrumental performances. It succeeds thrillingly, defying any dance purists who would argue that danceability is sacrificed on the altar of virtuosity.

The opening track, **Al Ver Sus Campos** establishes Barretto's Puerto Rican flag-waving credentials. Such a stance was de rigueur in the 1970s, and here it takes the form of a song about a *jibarito* (little country boy) surveying the land he no longer cultivates and the life he has lost, and weeping. Sentimentality is belied by the modernism of the arrangements: four trumpets, countered by a trombone and tenor, simply sweep you into a celebration of the *jibarito*'s new identity as a swinging, jazz-steeped New York musician. Little Adalberto may sing about what Puerto Rico has lost, but the band plays a dance-paced number of sublime sophistication.

What makes *Rican/Struction* so exciting is that it is a return to form after so much frustration. Barretto rightly believes that he was never given enough credit for pushing the bounds of salsa, and this album makes his case. Four progressive yet danceable salsa numbers – **Campos**, **Un Día Seré Feliz**, **Ya Vez** and **Adelante Siempre Voy** – are split by a truly wonderful bolero, **Piensa En Mí**, that shows off Adalberto's beautiful tenor and features an arrangement that echoes Gil Evans or Charlie Mingus. A vindication of Barretto's ambitions.

Then **Algo Nuevo** starts as a crisp danzón/cha-cha and flows seamlessly into a Latin-jazz big-band instrumental. Finally, a terrific descarga (jam session), **Tumbao Africano**, evokes Africa through ritual drum riffs with lyrics invoking the gods, then pushes on through to become a mini Latin-jazz suite. The Cuban maestros would have approved.

Tommy Garcia

Further listening: Mambo Mongo (Charly) is a magnificent example of Mongo Santamaría's illustrious Latin-to-jazz crossover career. Featuring 35 of the cream of Puerto Rico's musicians, **Descarga Boricua** (Tierrazo) is a seamlessly meandering tour de force of modern Latino jazz.

Jorge Ben Jor

Jor Ao Vivo

WEA Masters of Brasil, 1993

Jorge Ben Jor (vocals, guitar, percussion), Eduardo Helbourn (vocals, percussion), Ed Ferro (bass, vocals), Lori César (keyboards, vocals), Yosé Africano (percussion, vocals), Cassio Pioletto (violin), Sérgio Trombone (trombone), Bidinho (trumpet), Paulinho (trumpet), Zé Carlos (sax).

For Jorge Ben Jor, only a live album will do. No other Brazilian musician writes and performs such danceable music, a unique and seamless blend of Brazilian rhythms with Afro-American funk. Ben's music has remained pretty much unaltered since he first emerged in his native Rio de Janeiro in the late 1960s. Percussive and complex, with insanely catchy tunes and lyrics, his is the most infectious live act in Brazilian music. And at just over sixty years old, Ben still gets an audience on its feet like no other.

Jorge Ben, or Jorge Ben Jor (he changed his name in the 1980s), was born in Rio in 1940, and made his debut in the city's club scene in the 1960s. Like so many of the Brazilian stars who broke through in the 1960s and 1970s, he first got national exposure in Brazil's huge, televised song festivals. But as several of his contemporaries turned to American rock for inspiration, Jorge Ben began to draw on funk, mixing it with samba and the music of his Afro-Brazilian roots. Alongside his fellow *carioca* (someone from Rio), Tim Maia – listen for the shouted salute to him on **W/Brasil** – he pioneered the use of soul and funk in Brazilian music.

Unlike rock, which never did and never will sit easily with the subtle rhythms and versatility of the Brazilian musical imagination, the fit between funk and Ben's Afro-Brazilian beat is so close you can't see the seams. Everything is built around a tight percussion unit, with two sets of drums and an array of African and Brazilian percussion instruments. Tight brass sits over the fast, choppy rhythm, while Jorge's husky voice stretches phrases for the percussion to weave around, to hypnotic and riveting effect. The music is still quintessentially Brazilian, but the influence of George Clinton and Sly Stone is clearly discernible, as is the presence of early-1980s African funk, notably the West African highlife music of King Sunny Adé.

Jor Ao Vivo (Jor Live) was recorded in front of an ecstatic home audience in Rio in 1993, and represents Ben Jor at his peak. You don't hear much from the audience – they're too busy dancing. The album has all of the singer's showstoppers: **País Tropical** is a paean to Rio and Brazil in general, while **Spyro Gyro** is the essence of Ben Jor in that the constantly repeated two-line lyric makes no sense at all, but it doesn't matter. The funk anthem **W/Brasil** was Jor's biggest hit and became his signature tune. **Charles, Anjo 45** commemorates a shanty town bandit hero; and **Taj Mahal** is for anyone who ever wondered what ska sounded like speeded up. There is not a single pause for breath, not one slow number or drum solo, just unrelenting dance music.

Ben Jor's resolutely non-political lyrics meant he was one of the few major Brazilian stars to avoid trouble with the military censors in the 1970s. But at the 1971 song festival, the censors shut him down mid-performance for his double-entendre rendering of a song called **Give Me Soup**, and for the gyrations of the backing vocalists; he was accurately judged to be corrupting to minors. In his own way, he was – and is – more subversive than the most right-on political exile.

David Cleary

Further listening: Personalidade (Polygram) is a beautiful Jorge Ben
"Best of". Wagner Tiso's unusual **Wagner Tiso´s Brasil** (Caju)
has a jazz-fusion feel, in the style of Milton Nascimento.

Rubén Blades y Seis del Solar

Buscando América

Elektra/Asylum, 1983

Rubén Blades (guitar, vocals, percussion, composer), Mike Vinas (bass, guitar), Oscar Hernández (piano, keyboards), Eddie Montalvo (congas), Louie Rivera (bongos), Ralph Irizarry (timbales), Ricardo Marrero (vibraphone, synth, percussion).

A finger-clicking doowop chorus, all falsettos and deep bass-lines, opens **Buscando América** (Searching for America). Then Rubén Blades enters, singing "The ex-virgin hasn't decided what to do". It's the startling introduction to **Decisiones**, a story of a pregnant schoolgirl's dilemma, and hardly standard salsa fare. But then Rubén Blades is quite unlike anyone else in Latin music. He comes from Panama – rather than from the Spanish-speaking Caribbean islands or from New York, like most salsa singers – and he is a Grammy-winning singer and songwriter, a Hollywood movie actor, a Harvard lawyer and a politician. Blades has a reputation for telling tales from the streets of Latin America, but few releases were felt to be as shocking as this, his most controversial album. Nearly twenty years later, it still sounds as fresh and as relevant as when it first shattered the calm of 1980s salsa.

Buscando América was Blades' first solo album following the break-up of his staggeringly successful collaboration with Willie Colón. The two men had amassed gold discs and fame all over Latin America with a run of unconventionally brilliant albums, including *Siembra* (1978), the best-selling salsa record of the day. No-one expected anything ordinary, but *Buscando América* was a sensation, and remains a timeless collection of musical ideas drawn from all around the Americas – though the synthesizers give away its era.

The album's musical foundation is Cuban, but Blades weaves in reggae bass-lines and guitars, and rhythms from across Latin America – and sometimes loses sight of Cuba altogether. He also introduced a sleek new sextet called "Seis del Solar" (Six from the Block). Other salseros, including Colón, were still touring with full-strength dance orchestras, but Blades recreated the horns on synthesizers and added a kit-drum to the congas, bongos and timbales – a clue to his fascination with rock, in its hollow, echoey sound.

One refreshing feature of *Buscando América* is its variety. There is no unifying rhythm or arrangement, which is unusual for a salsa record. **Todos Vuelven** comes closest to conventional salsa. The song is an anthem – it still receives rapturous responses from audiences far away from home – and a showpiece for the sparkling vibes, which cruise at a cool pace while Oscar Hernández's rhythmic piano tags along to the bustle of the congas. The powerful, demanding monologue, **"GDBD"**, minutely documents a day in the life of "José average" in the *barrio* (neighbourhood), to a simple, bubbling backing of bongos. Blades next turns to life under the Latin American dictators of the 1980s: **Desapariciones** employs a sinister electronic drum tattoo to build the tension as he catalogues the cases of "the disappeared". **El Padre Antonio y el Monaguillo Andrés** marks the murders of nuns and priests in Central America's CIA-backed wars against the communists in the 1980s. It's an ironically lively, catchy song, driven by the swinging melody of the vibes and clattering percussion. Blades closes the album with a descarga, "searching for an America" which has been "kidnapped and gagged" while the band stretches delightfully into improvisational mode.

Sue Steward

Further listening: Colón and Blades' **Siembra** (Fania/Sonodisc) epitomizes radical 1970s salsa: a perfect blend. **Tiempos** (Sony Discos) is Blades' most radical album since Buscando América.

Carlinhos Brown

Alfagamabetizado

Virgin-EMI, 1996

Carlinhos Brown (vocals, percussion), and others; guests include Caetano Veloso, Gal Costa, Gilberto Gil, Maria Bethania, Marisa Monte (vocals).

Brazil's most prolific singer, songwriter, percussionist and producer is known by an assumed name. Inspired by the Godfather of Soul, Antonio Carlos added "Brown" (Carlinhos just means "little Carlos"), and today it is impossible to go anywhere in Brazil without hearing his music. Over the past decade, he has composed hundreds of hit songs and collaborated with artists from all over the country, including new Bahian stars such as Daniela Mercury and Marisa Monte, and even the giant rock group, Sepultura. Today, he is one of the leaders of a movement that takes traditional Afro-Brazilian drumming and sets it to a pop beat, adding electric guitars and a brass section. His trademark sound mixes funk, R&B, hip-hop, reggae and soul with the trademark drums of his hometown, Salvador de Bahia.

Salvador was Brazil's seat of government from 1549 to 1763, and today is the country's musical capital. For centuries, the Bahia region was the home of the Portuguese sugar industry – and the associated slave trade – and, as a result, it is one of the most important centres of African culture in the Americas. Amid the colonial architecture and cobblestone streets, the unmistakable beat of Bahian drumming blasts out of stereos and boomboxes playing the latest axé pop music. It becomes overwhelming when the large drumming ensembles – outfits such as Olodum,

Filhos de Gandhi, Ile Aiye and Timbalada – take to the streets. These groups, known as *blocos afros*, don't just have two or three drummers, but often hundreds.

Carlinhos Brown rose to prominence in the 1990s as leader of Salvador's mega-percussion ensemble Timbalada, whose one constant feature is the Bahian mix of Afro-Brazilian percussion with a touch of a reggae beat. In 1996, Brown took this Bahian samba-reggae in a completely new direction when he recorded **Alfagamabetizado**, a landmark album of Bahian music that brought together rock, MPB (Música Popular Brasileira), funk and samba-reggae with Brown' s unique percussive inventiveness. While the catchy pop hit **A Namorada** is well-known from its use on the *Speed 2* movie soundtrack, it hardly represents the vast spectrum of Brown's talent displayed on *Alfagamabetizado*.

On **Bog La Bag**, Brown uses his own voice as a percussion instrument. The song begins with the trademark Bahian beat, and then the vocal percussion kicks in: "Bog la bag la bog la bag la bog la bag la bog la bag la bo bla bla". This phrase repeats every three seconds and sets the base rhythm of a song that is shot through with Brown's irreverent sense of humour, percussive talent and Lenny Kravitz-like guitar riffs. On **Covered Saints**, Brown demonstrates his mastery of the Brazilian ballad, exquisitely balancing his dynamic vocal range with a restrained Afro-bloc chorus.

But perhaps the album's greatest achievement is **Seo Ze**, which opens delicately with Brown's *a capella* version of a cuica (squeaky drum). Conventional vocals and acoustic guitars enter next, to be joined by layer upon layer of sound, from Marisa Monte's haunting chorus to a salsa piano, building to the all-out finale of Timbalada's hundred-plus drum-and-chorus climax. *Alfagamabetizado* will become the standard by which the next generation of Afro-Brazilian albums will be measured.

David Cleary

Further listening: Yele Brazil (EMI-Hemisphere) **is a great compilation from 1990s Bahia, when blocos afros added brass sections and guitars to their sound. Mineral** (Polygram Brazil) **gives the real taste of Bahian carnival.**

Chico Buarque

Vida

Polygram Brasil, 1980

No musicians credited.

Chico Buarque was a surprise newcomer on the Brazilian scene in the 1960s. Seemingly overnight he emerged as the most lyrically brilliant *sambista* Rio had yet produced, and as a superb exponent of other traditional popular genres like choro and marcha. In the repressive 1970s, he was the most censored of all Brazilian stars, and wrote most of the best-remembered political protest songs of the period, including "Apesar de Você" (In Spite Of You) and "Vai Passar" (It Will Pass).

Throughout the 1980s and since he has consolidated his reputation, his lyrical genius causing him to be widely regarded as one of the best poets working in the Portuguese language. He is also a respected novelist, playwright and director, and his 1979 adaptation of Brecht and Weill's *Threepenny Opera*, its songs rewritten for a setting in 1940s Rio, was a landmark in the history of Brazilian theatre.

It seems surprising, then, that this symbol of cultural resistance was regarded as a political and musical conservative during the years of the military dictatorship. When he first emerged in the 1960s, his decision to work with traditional Brazilian popular forms was taken as a rejection of tropicalismo – the mixture of Brazilian and rock formats that had been pioneered by Gilberto Gil and Caetano Veloso and that was associated with criticism of the military regimes. For a period in the late 1960s, Buarque stood on one side and Veloso and Gil on the other in an almost

Beatles/Stones schism; Chico played music for nice kids while Caetano and Gil were the rebels. Yet when others were forced into exile, he kept the protest torch burning within Brazil, despite being forced into releasing albums of cover versions in the 1970s because so many of his own songs were censored.

Vida (Life) is one of a number of albums Chico released in quick succession in the late 1970s and early 1980s, as the political climate relaxed and he was at last able to put years' worth of previously banned songs into the public arena. They were a revelation to Brazilians who were mostly unprepared for the apparently sudden evolution of his talent after a decade of silence. The new Chico, while still working in traditional formats like samba, was also experimenting with jazzier, less traditional arrangements, typified on this album by tracks like **De Todas as Maneiras** and **Bye Bye Brasil**, the latter the signature tune to one of the finest Brazilian films of the 1970s.

Quoting extracts does his lyrics little justice, since they depend for their effect on the development of a theme over several verses, but even without a word of Portuguese it is possible to get some idea of the effect. On **Morena de Angola**, a song about watching an Angolan woman dance, his lyrics reach rich new levels of complexity, working a rush of rhyming syllables, African words and Portuguese words of African origin into the traditional samba form. Chico's light and slightly nasal voice is pleasant enough, if not in the same class as the voices of Caetano Veloso, Gilberto Gil or Milton Nascimento. But only Caetano comes close to Chico in his love for the Portuguese language or in his ability to play with words and meanings.

David Cleary

Further listening: Uma Palavra (RCA) reworks songs Buarque first recorded in the 1960s and 1970s. From the next generation, following in Buarque's footsteps, comes Marcio Faraco's **Cirando** (Emarcy). **Guitares du Brésil** (Harmonia Mundi) is a compilation of beautiful works by four living guitarists – Baden-Powell, Rosinha de Valença, José Barrense-Dias and Chiquinho Timoteo – including live and studio recordings.

David Byrne

Rei Momo

Luaka Bop/Sire, 1989

David Byrne (electric guitar, vocals) Johnny Pacheco (congas), Celia Cruz (vocals), Willie Colón (chorus, composer), and others.

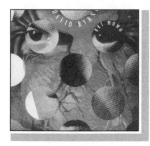

When David Byrne wearied of Talking Heads' rock-star life, he started visiting the places that gave birth to the music he listened to at home in New York. All through the 1980s, he would show up at the Village Gate's legendary "Salsa meets Jazz" nights and at the home of Brazilian music in exile, S.O.B.s (Sounds of Brazil), and he travelled extensively in Latin America. It was hardly surprising that when he launched the Luaka Bop label in 1989, Brazilian music and salsa figured large. But Byrne is no ethnomusicologist; he's a quirky futurist, a lover of fusion with his ear to the dance floor, and a songwriter with a whacky, inventive personal language.

His first venture into salsa was via the film director Jonathan Demme, who invited him to record a duet, **Loco de Amor**, with Celia Cruz for the soundtrack of his movie *Something Wild*. Cruz adopted an earthy, Afro-Cuban goddess role, chanting and scatting to a hypnotic Afro-Cuban percussion backing, weaving around Byrne's familiar, high-pitched, nasal voice (love it or hate it). **Rei Momo** came out a year later. Its lite-reggae beat and Cuban brass fit perfectly into the reconstructed Latin feel produced by veteran salsa supremo Johnny Pacheco.

Pacheco enlisted a super-group of musicians who created fifteen truly innovative songs. Virtually none are straight salsa – or even sámba, merengue or cha-cha-cha – but are infectious mutations of all those rhythms and more, passed through Byrne's distorting prism. *Rei Momo* received mixed reactions, but a decade later it is an essential fringe element of Latin music history.

The opening anthem, **Independence Day**, carries the cracked-voice charge and lurching rhythm of a Tex-Mex song, while **Office Cowboy** and **Don't Want To Be Part Of Your World** are full-bodied sambas. Other tracks are animated by Afro-Cuban percussion, led by Milton Cardona, José Mangual Junior and Marc Quiñones, the legendary trio which gave life to a score of influential albums by New York *salseros* such as Willie Colón and Rubén Blades. Pacheco didn't stint on brass or sax either, and they gorgeously embellish the itchy, twitchy merengues of **Call Of the Wild** and **Lie To Me**, which both rock to a throbbing tambora drum. **Dirty Old Town** features three blustery, dirty old 'bones, and three also dart around Mauricio Smith's crisp flute solo in **Women vs Men**, which sees Byrne concluding: "We're into sports, they're into flowers".

Byrne keeps his electric guitar on a close reign most of the time. On **Rose Tattoo** he crosses rock with Puerto Rican plena in a musical dance with Puerto Rican cuatro guitarist, Yomo Toro, and with **Good and Evil** he creates a rockster's feast to a jagged rumba beat. Eric Weisberg's pedal steel guitar playing in the cowboy-samba "Office Cowboy" is inspirational, and a foretaste of Ry Cooder's Havana experiments a few years later. Byrne makes no attempt to play the *salsero* (impossible, he hasn't the voice – or the hips), but succeeds because his songs are an honest and imaginative re-interpretation of the soundscape that fills his New York nights.

Sue Steward

Further listening: Songs from The Capeman (Warner Brothers), the soundtrack to Paul Simon's Broadway musical, is a collection of Simonisms blended with doowop, salsa, plena and Latin ballads, performed by the original cast, led by Rubén Blades and Marc Anthony. Marc Ribot y los Cubanos Postizos's **Muy Divertido** (Atlantic) sees the left-field New York guitarist on a set of tuneful transformations of Latin rhythms, Cuban to Mexican to Colombian, an adventurer's delight.

Cachao y Su Ritmo Caliente

Descargas – Cuban Jam Sessions

Egrem, 1996

Israel "Cachao" López (double bass), Guillermo Barreto (timbales), Tata Guines (congas), Rogelio Iglesias (bongos), Gustavo Tamayo (güiro), El Negro Vivar (trumpet), Generoso Jiménez (trombone), Orestes López (piano), Emilio Penalver, Virgilio Lesama (sax), Richard Egües (flute), Niño Rivera (tres guitar).

If you are born into a family with more than 35 bass players, including your mother, the chances are high that you'll play bass. So it was with Israel "Cachao" López, born in Havana in 1918, who test-drove piano, trumpet, tres and bongos before settling on bass. By the age of thirteen, he was playing in the Havana Symphony Orchestra – and he remained there for another 31 years, also performing with leading nightclub bands. At nineteen, he and his equally precocious brother, pianist Orestes, joined Las Maravillas del Siglo – later re-named Las Maravillas de Antonio Arcaño after the new bandleader. Their repertoire was danzones, elegantly swinging instrumentals flavoured by violins and sharp flute solos. The brothers provided Arcaño with nearly thirty new danzón compositions a week.

In 1938, Orestes wrote "Mambo", modernizing and Africanizing the danzón with an upbeat, syncopated tail section and creating the prototype for one of the world's great dance crazes. Conga drums eventually added extra rhythmic clout, and the interlocking rhythmic patterns between piano, bass and congas (the tumbao) formed a radical new rhythm skeleton. In 1954, Cachao – with flautist José Fajardo – presented the mambo at New York's Palladium dance hall and lit the touchpaper for years of mambo madness.

Before he left Cuba to live in New York in 1960, Cachao established the descarga tradition (literally, "letting go", but describing a "jam session") of group improvisations performed by top musicians after their nightclub shifts had finished. Originally released as singles, the tracks were collected together in the album *Descargas in Miniature*, which was first released in 1957. Fifty years later, released as **Descargas – Cuban Jam Sessions**, they remain magical masterpieces, peppered with rapid-response, ad-libbed solos.

Cachao's thick, velvety bass-lines threaded through each piece, offer a reassuring, web-like framework for the soloists. Whether tracing seamless notes from the chunky strings, or plucking light pizzicato, they are a constant focal point. In the spectacular opener, **Descarga Cubana**, he locks into an intriguing tumbao then trails reverberating melodies around the percussionists. **A Gozar Timbalero**, a rumba-like percussion workout, demonstrates the near-mystical rapport between bass and piano, conga and timbales. Orestes López's effortlessly rhythmic, staccato piano phrases and flowing melodies are heard here on **Oye Mi Tres Montuno**, while on **Cógele el Golpe**, Orestes flicks from syncopated Rachmaninov to son montuno, and in the deliciously upbeat **Malanga Amarilla**, drops in choppy mambo riffs.

These pieces are practically manuals on improvisation. Brass and percussion are exercised in **Goza Mi Trompeta**, where El Negro Vivar's striking trumpet is applauded in choruses of "*suena la trompeta!*" ("swing the trumpet!"), while **Sorpresa en Flauta** celebrates the danzón and cha-cha-cha era immortalized by Orquesta Aragón's spare, trilling flute solos.

In the US, Cachao continued the descarga tradition with the Alegre All Stars in the 1970s, and made scores of captivating solo albums. In 1994, Emilio Estefan and Cuban actor and conga player, Andy Garcia, produced the sensational *Cachao Master Sessions* albums, and immortalized the gentle genius in the moving biopic *Cachao – como su ritmo no hay dos* – for rhythm there is no rival.

Sue Steward

Further listening: Cachao Master Sessions, Volumes I and II (Crescent Moon/Sony) gave the eighty-something Cachao freedom to lavish his remarkable technique and repertoire on a new audience.

Café Tacuba

Re

WEA, 1999

Rubén Alvarín "Cosme" (vocals), Emmanuel del Real (keyboards), Joselo Rangel (guitar, jarana guitar), Quique Rangel (bass, toloche bass, guitarrón), and others.

Until the late 1980s, rock music in Mexico was the exclusive niche of an elite group of young, well-travelled people who bought imported recordings and devoured specialist music magazines. It was fuelled by a small but fanatical group of writers and fans with an encyclopaedic knowledge of R&B and alternative rock. Then, as the political climate changed and Mexico adopted what was called "Cactus Thatcherism", the doors opened to international bands. The Mexican bands that had been playing to small, appreciative audiences benefitted from the boom. Café Tacuba stood out, remaining at the top without commercializing themselves as pop stars, as did Maná and Los Caifanes.

Their trick was to transform the rich supply of Mexican traditional music – including son jarocho, son huasteco, norteño, banda and ranchera – with all the creativity and technical prowess of Los Lobos. They were never afraid of mixing country influences with urban rock in the same album (or even the same track), or of bringing a sharp irony and intelligence to all their different styles. A tremendous and very healthy irreverence runs throughout this record.

Re opens with **Aparato**, a track that introduces different elements from Mexican traditional music, including an impressive Huastecan falsetto from the band's lead vocalist, who brings a younger, fresher flavour to styles of music that have been rather exhausted by folk singers like Oscar Chavez. The second track, **La Ingrata**, is a harsh parody of the worst Mexican banda music – inane lyrics sung in a nasal pitch to a repetitive rhythm much appreciated by poor dancers.

El Fin de la Infancia opens with a few bars of Mexican brass band music, but urgently moves on to a harsher diet of urban rock. As the track closes there is hardly a second's pause before the band jolts into **Madrugal**, Café Tacuba's brief but respectful homage to the great Mexican romantic trios of the 1950s – though the lyrics stray far from the usual romantic platitudes towards comment on the current state of Mexico City.

Esa Noche is fairly straight international rock and far from what World Music fans expect from Mexico. The track is dedicated to the ranchera diva Chavela Vargas, as a tribute from the admiring band. It is one of the least irreverent tracks on a disc that doesn't let anyone else off lightly.

Re is filled with references to barrio heroes, street jargon, gay clubs, social abuses past and present, and the universal call of love and loss. The band use a combination of electronic and traditional instruments – including the small jarana guitar from Veracruz and the enormous guitarrón bass of the mariachi bands – to create a sound that is young and energetic but at the same time doesn't turn its back on older Mexican styles. They have a deep respect for the music they parody, and more than enough musical talent to play around it creatively.

As Café Tacuba move confidently through a great diversity of musical styles, calling in at Mexico's dance halls, country fiestas and cantinas, they present a vivid reflection of the country's complex everyday reality in which hard times and hope are always accompanied by music.

Mary Farquharson

Further listening: In Maldita Vecindad′s big-selling album, **El Circo** (BMG Ariola), Café Tacuba's biggest rival made a big impact on Mexico's younger audience. Among the younger generation, vocalist and composer Julieta Venegas is a strong contender for albums such as **Aquí** (BMG).

Cartola

Cartola

Discos Marcos Pereira, 1974

No musicians credited.

What is the best samba record ever? The question should keep people arguing for hours in a Rio bar, but in fact opinion in Brazil is pretty much unanimous – it's **Cartola**, by the *sambista* of the same name. Things are made slightly confusing by the fact that Cartola only made two records, both of which are called *Cartola* (the 1974 disc has a photo of the *sambista* on the cover, while the second, released in 1976, has a photo of Cartola and his wife). The two records were cut shortly before Cartola died, but he is to samba as Pelé is to Brazilian football – his life is the story of samba itself.

Cartola's real name was Angenor de Oliveira. He was born in a Rio slum in 1908, and grew up just as samba was forming itself into a recognized style. In 1928, already composing sambas, he was one of the founders of the first Carnival samba *escola* (school), Deixa Falar, which eventually became the main component of Rio's Carnival. Cartola moved on to become the founder of Mangueira, which evolved into Rio's largest and most famous samba school. Yet even with this pedigree, Cartola remained in obscurity. Like other black *sambistas* of the period he was barred from the Copacabana hotels, where the money was, and he made a precarious living selling sambas, many of which became classics, to white singers.

By the end of the 1930s Cartola had disappeared (though not before recording a track in 1932 called "Divina Dama"). He might never have been more than a footnote in samba's history, but amazingly, in the late 1950s, a samba historian discovered him washing cars for a living. Admirers such as Tom Jobim and Paulinho da Viola lent him enough money to start a small restaurant in central Rio in the 1960s, and Zicartola became one of the main places where samba musicians hung out. Eventually, Marcos Pereira, owner of a small studio, helped Cartola to make two records, of which this is the first.

There are no details of the musicians or vocalists, but they are people Cartola knew well – it's possible to hear them chatting at a couple of points. The sense of intimacy is revealed in the extraordinarily tight feel, the musicians effortlessly keeping pace with Cartola's loping, slightly hoarse voice – with a Rio accent you could cut with a knife. His immaculate phrasing and timing stretches bars and notes but always comes in perfectly on cue.

The songs are all less percussive than you might expect, harking back to Cartola's composing peak in the 1930s and 1940s, when samba was lighter and jazzier, making much greater use of instruments like the trombone and flute than modern samba. But the rhythm section here is fantastic, based not around drums but around tambourines, adding the reco-reco, a type of maraca, and the indescribable rasping whoop of the cuica, heard to particularly good effect on **Corra e Olhe O Céu** and **O Sol Nascerá**. The lyrics are universally melancholic, tears-of-a-clown love songs, counterpointing (not altogether convincingly) the upbeat, optimistic feel of the music. There is not a weak track, but if there is a highlight it is **Alvorada**, a beautiful, intimate samba greeting sunrise, co-written with another founder member of Mangueira, Carlos Cachaça, whose death in 1998 marked the passing of the last link with the early years of samba.

David Cleary

Further listening: the other Cartola (Discos Marcos Pereira)
includes Cartola's most famous samba, "As Rosas Não Falam".
Orfeo Negra (Verve) is the moving soundtrack to the 1950s film
Black Orpheus, a love story set in Rio´s favelas to music by
bossa nova creator Tom Jobim and guitarist Luis Bonfa.

David Calzado y
La Charanga Habanera

Tremendo Delirio

Magic Music/Universal, 1997

David Calzado (vocals), Leonel Polledo, Victorino Patterson, Osmil Monsón (trumpet), Jorge E. Maza (sax, flute), Victor Sagarra (congas), and others.

Representing a new, hedonistic generation of Cubans, David Calzado's Charanga Habanera found its moment of fame during the mid 1990s, when Cuba was emerging from the austerity created by the Soviet Union's withdrawal of financial support. A dramatic influx of dollar-bearing foreign tourists quickly transformed the island's nightlife, and stylish Calzado seized the imagination of Cuba's youth. His public celebration of all things consumerist – such as his open love of sports cars and finery – coupled with his highly sexual lyrics and personal profile brought him a young and adoring fan-base. He embraced the romantic ballads of US-based salsa with an over-the-top, catch-in-the-voice vocal style, while simultaneously drawing on Cuba's new, aggressively poly-rhythmic timba music.

Timba's driving power comes from modernizing the structure and rhythms of son, adding heavy, accented rumba grooves, rapped choruses and virtuoso jazz influences in rapid and complex brass arrangements. With a brace of acrobatic and exhibitionist dancers, Calzado openly challenged Revolutionary values. After the 1997 International Youth Festival, however – when he bragged on stage about smoking marijuana, apparently made double-edged jokes about Castro and dropped his trousers while encouraging tourists to cross an invisible line and mix with Cubans – Calzado was grounded by the government for six months. This in spite of a forthcoming, fully booked European tour. The group split in two, leaving Calzado forced to accept a lower profile at home for a while.

Each song on *Tremendo Delirio* focuses in different ways on the theme of sex for money and the complex impact this has had on personal relationships between Cubans themselves, and between Cubans and foreigners. The lyrics are highlighted by the intensity of the musical arrangements and by timba's associated dance, the pelota, which explicitly simulates either full sex or discreet, on-the-dance-floor masturbation.

The first track, **No Estamos Locos** (We're Not Crazy), blasting off with punchy brass and an intoned chorus, knocks you straight in the eye with the album's message: the soloist and chorus croon, "We're not mad/We know what we've got and what we want". Hip-hop percussion over bass chords leads into **Dime Que Te Quedarás** (Tell Me You're Staying), which captures everyday reality in a guy lamenting his girl going out to earn dollars – the chorus chanting that the Cuban ration book system died in the 1980s.

Calzado's lyrics are filled with up-to-the-minute slang that conjures vivid pictures of real situations, rather like video clips. **Un Disparo En La Mirada** (If Looks Could Kill) is replete with sexual metaphors, and likens attracting a woman's attention to overcoming her with a military arsenal. **Lola, Lola (Toque La Bola)** (Lola, Lola, Touch the Ball), with its choppy opening riffs, vocal rap and Caribbean drum sounds, uses baseball metaphors but carries extra resonance because "ball" is one of many slang terms for the dollar. **Hagamos Un Chen** (Let's Exchange) gets straight to the point: "how do you want to be paid, Mami? Cheque or cash?".

Jan Fairley

Further listening: Young singer Carlos Manuel's **Malo Cantidad** (Palm Pictures) took timba into a poppier boy-band world; the title track was a huge millennial hit in Cuba. Isaac Delgado's mellower, salsa romantica-tinged approach to timba can be heard on **La Fórmula** (Ahí Namá Music).

Willie Chirino

Oxígeno

Sony, 1991

Willie Chirino (bass, vocals, composer), Steve Roistein (synth), Tany Gil (congas), Wiso Santiago (drums), Sammy "Timbalón" Pagán (timbales), Juan J. Quiñones (trumpet, percussion), Miguel Romero (bass), Axel Ortiz (keyboards), Arturo Sandoval (trumpet).

Miami Beach's second show-business couple — after the Estefans — is Willie Chirino and his wife, Lisette. One is a mainstream balladeer, the other the creator of a distinctive, modern Miami salsa. Chirino, the musical magpie, built his sound around old Cuban music, new Cuban music, New York salsa, and Caribbean rhythms — soca, zouk, reggae — that he picked up off radio stations beaming in from the islands. They sweep through his songs like hot Miami breezes.

Like Emilio Estefan, Chirino arrived in Miami in his teens after Castro took control of Cuba, and began performing in the late 1960s. He switched from drums to electric bass after hearing Paul McCartney, and wore leathers and jeans in defiance of salsa's satins-and-flares. Miami's music scene then catered for his parent's generation in nostalgic songs about Cuba — songs from their youth that were irrelevant to young New Americans like Chirino and his friends. He competed for gigs at family parties and weddings with Emilio Estefan's Miami Latin Boys, but while Estefan went all the way in his flirtation with American music, Chirino stuck close to the Latin formula.

His live shows are joyful occasions, often brightened by the appearance of an (exiled) Cuban legend, passing through town. A regular flow of albums has revealed a man in constant change, picking up on trends in the Americas and fitting them to his own style. Chirino's sound depends partly on his soft, smooth, distinctive vocals, and partly on the tropical Caribbean influences he draws through the salsa. Its languor is very Miami. He added a drum kit and electronic drums before they were considered appropriate in a salsa band, but both are always answerable to the Cuban percussion at the heart of the music. His electric bass-lines soon abandoned McCartney's melodic poppiness after he heard Los Van Van's funk-influenced Cuban songo rhythms.

Oxígeno (Oxygen) is a delicious slice through a time when merengue was rampant in Latin America. Gentle, Juan Luis Guerra-style harmonies are heard on **Tengo**, but Chirino goes for the authentically crazed brassy sound in **La Noche Perfecta**. Chirino's merengues are always just a skip away from Trinidadian soca, whose calypso lilt pervades the album and dominates the opener, **Mister Don't Touch the Banana** – a very calypso title. In **Muévete, Muévete** (Move It, Move it), the most compulsive dance track, he introduces a zouk quality with the female choruses and a brisk snare drum. On the salsa-flamenca **Gitanilla**, Chirino's faint tremolo takes on a passable guttural warble, while the timbales add a sharp edge to the quick Andalucian guitar melodies and jumpy flamenco beat.

Most songs here are upbeat dancers or sensual love songs. But by 1991, Miami's musicians were beginning to enter the anti-Castro political arena. **Medias Negras** has the feel of Rubén Blades (if from the other side of the political barricades) in its precise, narrative vocal style and its simple backing of congas, piano and solo trumpet. **Nuestro Día (Ya Viene Llegando)** even drops in a provocative fragment of the "Red Flag" chorus, which is soon over-ruled by chants of "Libre!" (Free!). The album closes with the words "Cuba! Our day will come!".

Sue Steward

Further listening: Willie Chirino's **Cuba Libre** (Sony) draws on a nostalgic repertoire worthy of Buena Vista to state its opposition to Castro's Cuba. The commercially appealing salsa of Miami's harmonizing vocal duo, Hansel y Raúl, can be heard on **Celebrando** (Sony Tropical).

Willie Colón and Héctor Lavoe

Lo Mato – Si No Compra Este LP

Fania, 1973

Willie Colón (trombone), Héctor Lavoe (vocals), Santi González (bass), José Mangual (bongos), Luis Romero (timbales), Joe Torres (piano), Eric Matos (trombone), Milton Cardona (congas), and others.

Tito Puente called the first records by Willie Colón and Héctor Lavoe "kiddy music", but their passion, honesty and punkish amateurism sang out to young NuYoricans, and made them superstars. The pair worked together from 1967 until 1974, though Colón produced several subsequent albums for Lavoe – including the singer's last, just before his death in 1993. Colón moved on to a more complex partnership with Rubén Blades which brought the pair million-selling records, awards and some of salsa's most lasting songs. Today, Colón is an elder of US salsa.

When *El Malo* appeared, the trombonist, songwriter and leader, Willie, was 17 and the singer, Héctor, was 21. The album established a rather unconvincing hoodlum image that lasted over several releases. Salsa elders shuddered at their music; few things were more precious than the Cuban Tradition, and the mostly self-taught members of Colón's gang were clearly rule-breakers. But *El Malo*'s intense songs about everyday experiences chimed with young Latinos, and Lavoe's startlingly mature voice - fired with passion, stained with melancholy, and bearing the appealing nasal edge of the great Puerto Rican vocalists - was irresistible. Their live shows were as riotous as concerts by The Beatles.

Lo Mato – Si No Compra Este LP (I'll Kill Him – If You Don't Buy This LP) appeared in 1973, and Colón was obviously listening to new influences. **La María**, for instance, is a gorgeously swinging confection of swishing samba rhythms and salsa that, thirty years later, still insinuates its way into hips and feet. Written by Puerto Rico's most significant songwriter, Tite "Curet" Alonso, it reflects Colón's discovery of the Brazilian music that has infused his sound ever since.

Lavoe left behind many great solo albums, but this early collaboration with Colón is an unpolished beauty. The straight-ahead salsa of **Señora Lola** and **Vo So** allows him to work his vocal magic, while the immortal **Calle Luna, Calle Sol**, a cautionary tale about muggers in Old San Juan, sees him in wonderfully open voice. Lavoe advises seeking protection from the saints, while Colón creates a dance track from an anxious, stop-start rhythm built with trombones and percussion.

A more loping, street-band effect is achieved on **Todo Tiene Su Final**, which is enlivened by "El Profesor" Joe Torres's fluid and precisely rhythmic piano. Another dance-floor classic, **El Día De Suerte**, canters like a horse through the Puerto Rican countryside to a traditional, bumpy bomba rhythm. Propelled by Milton Cardona's bubbling congas and José Mangual's pin-sharp bongos, it also evokes jangling bridlery in triangle and bells. A squeaky Brazilian cuica drum lurks in the mix, while trombones play the angular choruses which became Colón's catchphrase.

Colón's devotion to his family's home island is reinforced by Yomo Toro's traditional Puerto Rican cuatro guitar, which gives another helping of the nostalgic scent of the countryside, particularly on the energetically rural **Guajira Ven**. But the Colón sound is dominated by trombones - the instrument he learnt aged fourteen, after abandoning the trumpet. He snorts and flows and rages, and sometimes awkwardly negotiates melodies which he probably could imagine but couldn't fully achieve. The result is rough diamond magic - pure punk-salsa.

Sue Steward

Further listening: Colón's sweet **Criollo** (RCA) ventures into Caribbean, Puerto Rican and Brazilian music. Lavoe's **La Voz** (Fania) was his first solo album, adding trumpets to the trombones backing his emotive voice.

Manny Oquendo y su Conjunto Libre

Ritmo, Sonido y Estilo

Montuno, 1983

Manny Oquendo (timbales, bongos, güiro), Andy González (bass), Jerry González (congas, trumpet), Joe Mannozzi, Oscar Hernández (piano), Dan Reagan, Jimmy Bosch, Steve Turre, Reynaldo Jorge, Papo Vázquez (trombone), Dave Valentín (flute), Pupi Cantor Torres, Hermán Olivera (vocals).

Conjunto Libre's co-founders, Manny Oquendo and Andy González, have a fanatical and almost mystical belief that their music has a mission, at the very least cultural and perhaps even transcendental. New Yorkers born to Puerto Rican parents, they believe their music should be the most honest manifestation of that Latin identity. And since the group's foundation in 1974, theirs has been almost a siege mentality against "Anglo" culture, defending the Caribbean roots of their music, as they see it, by reinterpreting it, drawing on the cornucopia of musical styles that find expression around them. They were pioneers, and today are keepers of that intense, perhaps now flickering, flame loosely known as New York salsa.

Over the years, musicians have queued to play with Libre, and it came to be known as an academy of Caribbean Latin music. Flautist Dave Valentín, an original member who has recorded over thirty albums as a solo artist, insists he learnt to time his solos by listening to Manny Oquendo. Great players have passed through its ranks, each understanding and contributing to the trade-off between the energy of keen, raw talent and the superbly engineered vehicle it fuels.

Ritmo, Sonido y Estilo (Rhythm, Sound and Style) is a perfect album. Six tunes, all classics in their way, benefit from bravura arrangements that range from breath-expelling excitement to melting tenderness. And Libre have the confidence and aplomb to carry off extended numbers that still leave one impatient for more. For some years after its release in 1983, it looked as if Libre would not record again. The complexity of keeping together a group of musicians of such calibre and ambition in New York, notably in the face of an increasingly commercialized industry indifferent to their perfectionism, militated against Libre's wider success. They became almost the music's best kept secret, with *Ritmo* their monument.

Libre's immense and undervalued contribution lies in their trademark expansive arrangements. A marvellously melancholic version of the Cuban guaracha rhythm on **Qué Humanidad**, a lament for human nature, is liberated midway by the chorus singing "*Somos libre de verdad*" ("We are truly free"). Are they rejoicing in being *libre* (free) or Libre? The gloriously smooth ride of the trombones on **Bentley** is strictly Continental, while **Báilala Pronto** is a mambo that draws on Libre's dance roots as skilfully as Freddie Hubbard's jazz standard, **Little Sunflower**, is sumptuously Latinized.

The plena, a driving Puerto Rican rhythm, is given a new dimension on **Elena, Elena**, as the band progresses from the opening scrap-metal percussion outbreak to an edge-of-your-seat series of ensemble sections. Just as you've recovered your breath, Jimmy Bosch's Creole trombone powers a solo to knock it out of you again, while Manny Oquendo takes a timbales solo that manages to both propel the arrangement and be measured, tuneful and tense. The overall catchiness and freshness of the groove have made this album a perennial favourite with dancers, who are put through their paces blissfully unaware of the subtle complexity that motivates them.

Tommy Garcia

Further listening: Estrellas Caiman's **Descarga Brava 2000!** (Caimán) features Oquendo and González within a New York jamming group of frightening pedigree. For yet more swinging, hard salsa, reach for Libre alumnus Jimmy Bosch's **Soneando Trombón** (Ryko Latino).

Gal Costa

Acústico (Unplugged)

RCA/Victor, 1997

Gal Costa (vocals), Wagner Riso, João Rebouças (piano), Jurim Pereira (drums),
Jorge Oscar (electric bass), Mou Brasil (guitar), Zé Canuto (saxophone, flute),
Sidinho Moreira (percussion), Jorge Soares, Ricardo Cândido, João Anunciação,
Sônia Zanon (bass).

Gal Costa has been at the very apex of the Brazilian music scene since the 1960s and, like her great contemporaries Caetano Veloso, Gilberto Gil and Chico Buarque, seems if anything to be getting better with age. Although she possesses one of the very finest voices of any Brazilian singer, extraordinarily pure and sensuous, she has never quite been thought of as the leading female singer of her time. In her early career, she saw that title go to Elis Regina, who was technically not as good as Costa but able to project a depth of emotion unmatched by any of her peers. More recently, she has been overshadowed a little by the brilliance of Marisa Monte. All the same, she is a superb singer and a matchless interpreter of classic Brazilian music from the so-called "golden age" of the 1930s and 1940s.

Costa was also at the cutting edge of the tropicalismo movement of the 1960s, a groundbreaking eclectic jumble of Brazilian genres and rock. Her 1968 album, *Tropical* (not yet released on CD), was a classic *tropicalista* manifesto, veering between electric rock and styles from Bahia, her home state in Brazil's northeast. The record made her a national star, a position she has never lost, and her frequent international tours have made her one of the best-known Brazilian stars abroad as well.

This live album is a great retrospective, and the acoustic setting and lush string backing are the perfect accompaniment to Costa's dreamy, sensuous and perfectly controlled voice. She is particularly closely associated with her Bahian peers, Caetano Veloso and Gilberto Gil, especially Caetano, and the opening four tracks on this album – four of the biggest hits of her career – are all Veloso compositions. The fifth, **Voca Não Entende Nada**, just as big a hit, also dates from the 1960s. The gorgeous love song, **Baby**, is a particularly appropriate opening track; it pulls Brazilians of her generation back to the late 1960s with the same force as a classic Motown hit does for American contemporaries.

Great though these more modern highlights of her career are, they are matched by a well-chosen group of songs by older Brazilian composers, especially Ary Barroso, the *sambista* who took samba to a new level of musical and lyrical sophistication in the 1940s. Costa recorded *Aquarela do Brasil*, an entire album of Ary Barroso songs, in 1980, and the two tracks covered here, **Aquarela do Brasil** and **Camisa Amarela**, give an idea of how good it is. **Falsa Baiana**, written by Barroso's friend and contemporary Geraldo Pereira, also belongs to this group. They combine great melodies with fine lyrics, and the string-dominated arrangements perfectly set off their 1940s feel.

Another group of songs on this album is more contemporary, and show how Costa's talent is still maturing. The best example is the haunting **Vapor Barato**, written by the young singer Zeca Baleiro in 1996, which is about unsuccessfully trying to forget an obsessive love affair. Costa's voice slides around Zeca's, pulling an ordinary melody into something more powerful, and bordering on disturbing. As Gal Costa approaches her sixties, she is still capable of giving rivals less than half her age a lesson in vocal grace, control and power.

David Cleary

Further listening: Aquarela do Brasil (Philips) is a superb, seductive collection of Ary Barroso songs from the 1930s and 1940s, perfectly arranged and sung. Fellow tropicalista, Maria Bethânia, just missed out on the final cut for the hundred CDs; **Alibi** (Polygram) glories in her sensual contralto voice.

Celia Cruz

On Fire – The Essential Celia Cruz

Manteca, 2000

Backed by La Sonora Matancera, and bands led by Johnny Pacheco and Tito Puente.

The Cuban Queen of Salsa, the supreme Latin American Diva, and one of the world's vocal wonders, Celia Cruz, first sang in public over half a century ago on Havana radio. Since then, her songs have found their way into the hearts of fans all over the world, and her sensational, effervescent performances are an inspiration and a revelation. For exiled Cubans she is something approaching a deity.

Cruz's rags-to-riches story began in 1930s Havana, when she won a radio talent contest that led to gigs at Havana's leading nightclubs. In 1951, bandleader Rogelio Martínez hired her to sing with his outstanding Afro-Cuban dance band, La Sonora Matancera. Their brand of modernized son, guaracha, guajira and rumba, and their tear-stained boleros, were among the most exciting on the bill at many top Havana nightspots all through the heady, pre-Revolutionary 1950s. After the Revolution, their success continued in Mexico City and New York, where La Celia was the jewel in the band's crown.

Celia stayed with La Sonora Matancera until 1963, and their recordings together remain some of her most perfect – the majority of songs on this compilation date from that time. The assured young singer had a wide range of octaves to play with, and gloried in darting around them with the fluidity of an operatic singer – though she could also turn rich, throaty and downright dirty. **Rico Changüi** resurrects the old changui rhythm, with La Celia adopting a strident tone as the percussionists drive a forceful, syncopated pace (while sounding as if they were recorded in an old shed). Celia possesses an intuitive skill with rhythm, exemplified as she masters the dramatic rhythmic changes in Cuban songs like **Cao, Cao, Maní Picao**, her first recording for Martínez. A decade on, with New Yorker Johnny Pacheco, she ad-libs on the immortal tongue-twister, **Químbara**, at what Pacheco described as "computer speed".

La Sonora Matancera was a cohesive collection of soloists who got too little solo exposure on record. Pianist Lino Frías occasionally deserts his function as rhythm anchorman and shines through with a sparkling solo, as on the sensually shuffling **Suavecito**. **Cha Cha Guere** generates exciting tension by alternating vocal choruses and high-pitched trumpets with Celia's playful lead lines. Another key soloist, trumpeter Pedro Knight, is in spectacular, high-pitched abandon on the pumping Puerto Rican bomba, **Mi Bomba Sonó**, while Cruz, who was to become his wife, is at her most vocally agile.

In the 1960s, Celia embarked on a long partnership with percussionist and bandleader Tito Puente – represented here on **En el Tiempo de la Colonia**. In 1974, La Reina made her debut album with Johnny Pacheco, *Celia and Johnny*, which brought them a gold disc and gave Cruz a slew of hits-for-life. Among such treasures are **Cúcala** – quintessential Pacheco with its jumpy, itchy rhythms and sharp, bitter-sweet trumpets.

Such songs have brought pleasure to millions. Today, Doña Celia's voice is understandably narrower, and her energy a tad diminished, making compilations like this one even more precious.

Sue Steward

Further listening: La Sonora Matancera Live on Radio, 1952–1958 (Harlequin/Interstate) is a sensational record including extended instrumental solos and some of the band's exceptional vocalists. Cruz's **Mi Vida Es Cantar** (RMM/Sony) showcases 1990s New York salsa, with plenty of contemporary Cuban influences.

Cubanismo In New Orleans

Mardi Gras Mambo

Hannibal/Rykodisc, 2000

Jesús Alemány (leader, trumpet), Rolo Martínez, Rafael Duany (vocals), José Jeréz (trumpet), Carlos Alvarez (trombone), Jorge Maza (flute), Efraín Ríos (tres, guitar), Nachito Herrera (piano), Robèrto Riverón (bass), Yosvany Terry (alto sax), John Boutté (vocals), and others.

Cross-cultural collaborations are all the rage in projects as diverse as Tuvan-Bulgarian and Japanese-Jamaican, but sadly, what makes for a riotous basement session more times than not ends up sounding like musical road-kill. Cubanismo's **Mardi Gras Mambo** stands out as one of the best musical hybrids in years. But then the idea of linking New Orleans jazz and funk with Cuban son, mambo and rumba isn't such a step in the dark. Before Castro and the US embargo, Havana and New Orleans were linked as the two musical capitals of the Caribbean. Musicians would hop between Miami, Havana, New Orleans and other spots, and new musical styles sprang up throughout the Caribbean as a result of the dynamic mix of Spanish, French, indigenous, and African cultures – styles which shaped American Jazz as much as Cuban popular music.

Cubanismo's bandleader, Jesús Alemány, is regarded by some as one of the greatest trumpeters and bandleaders in the world. Three years after leaving the Guillermo Tomás conservatory in Havana – at the age of thirteen – he joined the critically acclaimed son innovators, Sierra Maestra, who led a Cuban son revival. One decade and eleven releases later, Alemány set out to carve his own musical path. He formed Cubanismo, an all-star fifteen-piece Cuban orchestra. Whether they are playing guajira, son, mambo or descarga jam-sessions, Cubanismo has the near magical effect of getting the most leaden-footed gringos onto the dance floor. Alemány's trademark was creating descargas with space for mesmerizing brass solos, while keeping the songs first and foremost danceable. The group led the "Cuban musical invasion" of the US and Europe in the 1990s, with their best-selling debut release, *Cubanismo* (Hannibal).

Mardi Gras Mambo is a departure from Cubanismo's usual Cuban descarga-filled albums. For this recording, Alemány went to New Orleans, a city regarded as the "northernmost point in the Caribbean", and the resulting sessions were a magical mix of genres rooted in Africa and developed in the Americas – Cuban son, mambo, cha-cha-cha, danzón and salsa, blended with New Orleans R&B, jazz, boogie, blues, and Mardi Gras Indian chants.

The opening track, **Marie Laveaux**, is a tribute to Louisiana's legendary voodoo queen. New Orleans crooner John Boutté and Cuban vocalist Rafael Duany flawlessly trade verses in Spanish and English. It's a magical mix of blues and salsa so infectious that if you didn't know that this was a new project, you'd think you were listening to a decade-old genre dubbed something like "swamp salsa". Another number which stands out is the ambitious **Shallow Water Suite**, on which Alemány brilliantly brings together a variety of traditions, ranging from southern gospel, jazz, Cuban rumba, and the music of the "Black Carnival Indians", the feathered associations that take to the streets of New Orleans during Mardi Gras.

From the danzón inspired **It Do Me Good**, to Boutté's soulful English-language bolero, **Nothing Up My Sleeve**, the album is full of gems. It sounds remarkably fresh, due in large part to the production of Jesús Alemány, Mark Bingham and Hannibal's Joe Boyd, who demonstrate that these two musical hot-spots are musically linked, despite the political walls.

Dan Rosenberg

Further listening: Cubanismo's earlier recordings, **Cubanismo** and **Melembe** (both Hannibal/Rykodisc), reveal exquisite Cuban descarga, guajira, son and mambo, with an all-star cast and some wonderful guests.

21

Oscar D'León

Los Oscares de Oscar

Top Hits Records, 1996

No musicians credited.

Venezuela never figured large on the salsa map, but the singer Oscar D'León is not only Venezuela's premier performer, he is arguably one of the greatest living *salseros* (salsa performers). The "Lion of Salsa", as this tall, hunky fifty-something is known, carries one of the most professional, light-hearted and sexy road shows. He creates an atmosphere of relentless excitement, barely allowing audiences to pause for breath as his orchestra tears through the playlist. He is a reckless, charismatic entertainer, a great dancer and a powerful singer in the tradition of the great salsa tenors.

This compilation is a record of hits from his time with Dimensión Latina (1972–76), and from his own spectacular, trombone-dominated 1980s line-ups, the bands which introduced him to the wider world. With Dimensión Latina, he perfected the art of singing and playing whilst dancing with his bass. In his own band, he established a three-trombone, melody-carrying block, often augmented by three trumpets for a change in texture and balance. He employed a bassist, Daniel Silva, and concentrated on fronting the band, but still took occasional solos – and would always dance with his virginal, all-white electric bass.

Oscar D'León's first hit, **Llorarás**, is an essential at every show. He plays the high-pitched, pleading lover (not very convincingly) as the trombones reiterate his lead melody – an effective device. Many songs recreate scenarios between men and women, raising cheers from both sexes in the audience. The delicious **Los Tamalitos de Olga** (Olga's buns), a love story about a street trader – with obvious alternative meanings – sees the piano simulate the jangly Cuban tres guitar while the trumpets and trombones take the flute part. The choruses, sung in the whiney, nasal "old lady" style characteristic of Cuban son, are marvellously infectious.

For classic 1980s salsa, D'León is unbeatable. Chunky congas and spiky bongos drive **Liberate**, and trumpets tangle with trombones; the Lion himself is in salsa-balladeer mode, while the pianist's lively, jazzy solo recalls Papo Lucca. **Poco a Poco** is a tribute to the pleasures of dancing – cha-cha-cha redressed as brassy, late 1980s salsa. **Que Se Sienta** is a confession about a lover's tactile charms, exercising the high, passionate spectrum of the singer's voice. The heavy impact of three trombones firing in unison opens **Siéntate Ahí**, whose choruses imitate a girl's cries – but sound more like a goat.

In choosing to cover **Calculadora**, D'León hooked into Cuba's musical history. Although originally created by the pioneering cha-cha-cha purveyors, Orquesta Aragón, D'León chooses to imitate the tougher re-worked version by his idol, Beny Moré. D'León is at his most carefree: great swoony violin melodies and a bobbing pizzicato distract from the fast, sinuous rhythm that is spelled out on the güiro and carried on every instrument to create a sensational, sensuous experience. An unusual air of reflection pervades **A Él** (To Him), a homage to the singer's father, his working-man's hands and hard life. The tone is echoed in sombre trombone choruses. But the irrepressible Lion springs back in old-fashioned Afro-Cuban style with Miguelito Valdés's 1950s hit, **Rumba Rumbero** – and leaves you crying out for more.

Sue Steward

Further listening: Combinación Perfecta (RMM/Sony) features duets by the leading salseros of the 1990s and sees D'León pitched with Celia Cruz and José Alberto. **Sangre Negra** (Sony) is fresh, clean salsa from Orlando Poleo, whose voice resembles that of his fellow Venezuelan, D'León.

22

Dark Latin Groove

Swing On

Sony, 1997

Huey Dunbar, James "Da' Barba" Jesús, Wilfrido "Fragrancia" Crispín (vocals), Sergio George (keyboards, drum programming, composer), Rubén Rodríguez (bass), Robert Vilera (timbales, bongos), Richie Flores (congas), Alejandro Odio (trumpet), Ozzie Meléndez (trombone), Kimo Solís (güiro, maracas), and others.

Hip-hop began to infiltrate the Latin charts in the late 1980s, inspired by the success in 1988 of two 12-inch singles from New York: "Set fire to me", by veteran *salsero* Willie Colón, and Amoretto's "Clave Rocks". Both blended electro-disco with salsa, stoked with "live" instruments – Tito Puente, no less, played with Amoretto. A decade later, a genuine new expression of bi-cultural Latin youth emerged with Proyecto Uno's *New Era*, rooted in merengue and rap, and Dark Latin Groove, the project of prolific Grammy-winning salsa producer Sergio George. Dark Latin Groove's debut album, *DLG*, was peppered with Sergio George trademarks, its title song reflecting a passion for Cuban timba in its deep, dragging bass lines, jolting rhythms and stuttery, driving horn phrases.

Of the three members of DLG, only James "Da' Barba" Jesús had any experience of salsa. Huey Dunbar, a good looker with a soulful falsetto, was spotted in a talent contest and given lead position. He spoke Spanish; the others took classes. Wilfrido "Fragrancia" ("Fragra") Crispín, singer and rapper, arrived from the influential mereng-rap duo Sandy y Papo. George produced eight songs for their milestone debut album, which quickly turned the trio into boy-band pin-ups with a record in the charts.

A year after *DLG*, **Swing On** shot into the charts. This time, as well as the timba effects, George also incorporated Jamaican dancehall and thunderous Puerto Rican bomba beats into the mix. And, of course, he punctuated it with growling, prowling raps. His own rhythmic Cuban piano style underlies most songs. The opener is a late-1980s classic reinvented for twenty-first century dance floors: **La Quiero a Morir** was a monster hit for the merengue balladeer Sergio Vargas, but DLG's version is carried on those tempting timba trumpets, and what starts as a pensive love song is brightened as the backing fills out. The album's ballads introduce young Latino soul-stirrer Cyndi Davila, whose duets with Dunbar are a well-matched blend, particularly on **La Soledad**, where the salsa is prised apart for a reggae break with softly booming bass-lines. On **Lágrimas** (Tears), they stand back as Fragra enters a dub zone – piano, brass and bass switched to Jamaican time in a slow-burning Latino-reggae rap.

Magdalena, Mí Amor (Quimbara) reveals the producer's magpie tendencies. Racing choruses, constructed from the Celia Cruz classic, "Quimbara", alternate with the verses, accompanied by what sounds like samba drumbeats. Fragra and Da' Barba join New York's Queen Ivy in freewheeling raps, then Dunbar swans back in on a wavering, flamenco-flavoured solo. The club favourite – another revamp – is **Juliana**, a hit in the 1960s for Dominican salsa icon, Cuco Valoy. Dunbar and Valoy recreated the recording in a spectacular live version at the group's farewell concert in New York in 1999. As knickers landed on stage around the singers, and girls shed tears over Huey's departure, Sergio George beamed from his keyboards as the two falsettos – one rich and mature, the other sweet and youthful – shared Valoy's memories of a lost love. DLG were a short-lived phenomenon, but their three albums paved the way for a generation of music-makers reared on hip-hop but also dancing salsa.

Sue Steward

Further listening: Fulanito's **El Padrino** (Cutting Records) brilliantly develops young Latino music's clash of Spanglish hip-hop and merengue. Sancocho's **Rumba Te Tumba** (Cutting Records) is the NuYorican treatment of the same Fulanito/DLG concept.

23

Gloria Estéfan

Mi Tierra

Sony/Epic, 1993

Gloria Estéfan (vocals, composer), Emilio Estéfan Jr. (composer, producer), Israel "Cachao" López (bass, cello), Tito Puente (timbales), Sheila E. (congas, timbales), Paquito D'Rivera (sax), members of Miami Sound Machine, the London Symphony Orchestra, and others.

Gloria Estéfan is the jewel in the Cuban–American crown, but until this 1993 release she had never recorded a true Latin album. That year, she and her producer-husband Emilio paused from cranking out million-selling rock hits with a Latin tinge, and turned to the Cuban music of their childhood.

They hooked up musicians from their band, Miami Sound Machine, with the cream of Miami's Cuban musicians, emerging with twelve surprising songs with a strong emphasis on the son style which *Buena Vista Social Club* eventually made world-famous. **Mi Tierra** was bought by people who had danced to the Miami Sound Machine's classics, "Conga!", "Rhythm's Gonna Get You" and "1-2-3", without knowing anything about salsa.

Estefan sang in Spanish throughout this album, and nothing she sang in English afterwards ever sounded so good. In the ballad, **Mi Gran Amor**, her voices warms like olive oil in sunshine and she positively basks in the enfolding guitar melodies. Supporting her are an awesome list of pioneers and instrumental virtuosi who represent several eras of Cuban music, from eighty-something double bass player and mambo inventor, Israel "Cachao" López, to New York's "Mambo King", Tito Puente, and saxophonist Paquito D'Rivera, who fled Havana and the revolutionary Afro-Cuban jazz group Irakere. From Miami they hired the seriously talented flautist, Nestor Torres, ubiquitous tres guitarist, Nelson González, and Paquito Hechavarría, whose piano solo lit up Miami Sound Machine's "Conga!".

The record opens poignantly with the ballad **Con Los Años Que Me Quedan**, conjured in the wake of the Estéfans' tour-bus accident a few years earlier. The party begins with the upbeat title track, a modernist son which targets American-Cuban exiles with buzz-words evoking a lost homeland: "The land where you were born you can never forget because it holds your roots and everything you've left behind...". The nostalgic son theme continues in Juanito Márquez's **Montuno**, with its jangly, metallic tres guitar and the incongruous but appealing soca horns, set to images of horse-drawn carts and sugar cane fields. In contrast to the pervasive guitars-and-trumpets formula and jaunty rhythm, **No Hay Mal Que Por Bien No Venga** is a gloriously old-fashioned danzón – the dignified dance with trilling flute solos and soaring violins – accompanied by the London Symphony Orchestra. It is a showcase for Cachao's husky, reverberating bass-lines, which hold the group together. The singer climbs down an octave to match the mood.

Politics inevitably make an appearance: **Hablemos El Mismo Idioma** (Let's Speak The Same Language), backed by a feast of guitars, flute and horns, is a pan-Latin anthem to "freedom", though not specifically addressed to Cuba. The set closes with **Tradición**, a celebratory number which poses Gloria Estéfan her greatest challenge – to sing Afro-Cuban guaguancó rumba, a genre traditionally improvised to drums. The modern arrangements, supported by a lattice of Cachao's basslines and Puente's clashing timbales, make the task less daunting, and Estéfan rises to it perfectly, as if lifted by the song's sentiments.

Sue Steward

Further listening: Gloria Estéfan adopts a richer, deeper, quasi-Nashville twang on **Abriendo Puertas** (Sony/Epic), which turned from Cuban son to Colombia's upbeat, accordion-led vallenato style for its inspiration.

Estrellas de Areito

Los Héroes

World Circuit, 1999

Rafael Bacallao, Teresa García Caturla, Miguelito Cuní, Carlos Embale, Manuel Furé, Tito Gómez, Filiberto Hernández, Pío Leyva, Pepe Olmos, Magaly Tars (vocals), and the roll-call of key Cuban musicians.

"Stars of Areito" is one of the most exceptional Cuban recordings of the twentieth century, a veritable Who's Who of musicians embracing three generations and ten key bands. Every track is uniquely scintillating. In 1979, Cuba's national label, Egrem, set aside five recording days in their studios in Havana for a special super-group encounter. Producer and trombonist Juan Pablo Torres captured Cuban music's improvisatory spirit by establishing the first part of each track as a simple melody using Cuba's son or guajira forms, then letting the second section, called the montuno, flow into a free descarga (jam session). Each number was recorded "live", in one take.

The fourteen astonishing tracks are remarkable for the quality of musicianship, the warm rapport between the players, the varied timbre and texture of the sounds, and the extraordinary number of Cuban musical forms alluded to. Responses between the musicians are full of joyful surprise and they spur each other on without fear of being eclipsed. The line-up included most of the key innovators of Cuba's classic dance forms and they shared a long history of both formal performance and casual late night jazz jamming. It's a pedigree particularly poignant in the spirited contributions of violinist Rafael Lay, singer Miguelito Cuní and trumpeter Félix Chappotín, who all died within the next five years, and in the work of ace trumpeter Arturo Sandovál and saxophonist Paquito D'Rivera, who left Cuba shortly after the recording. No track runs at less than six minutes, and some extend to fourteen – making for a true feast.

The original idea for the project came from Ivory Coaster, Raúl Diomandé, who is celebrated in Pedro Aranzola's opening number, **Póngase Para Las Cosas**, sung by the inimitable Pío Leyva (now a key member of the Afro-Cuban All Stars). Diomandé's hand is evident in the laid-back opening of the punchy brass chorus and also in the subsequent track, **Hasta Pantijo Baila Mi Son**, featuring Rubén González's choppy piano vamps and Miguel Barbón's violin. **Mi Amanecer Campesino** is a jewel: introduced by plonky guitar over a piano functioning as a "walking bass", it brings in soloist Pío Leyva partnered by rising blasts of tenor brass over an African-sounding tres guitar. The shifting timbres of Pedro Hernández's violin evoke rural animal and bird sounds, as do Niño Rivera's country-style finger-picked solos on the tres. Rubén González's percussive piano playing, heard on many tracks, sustains the whole.

Apart from a duet with Magaly Tars on **Para Mi Cuba Traigo Un Son**, Teresa García Caturla is the only woman taking part. She acts as a foil to the men on **Fefita,** which kicks off with engagingly muted brass solos, then adds Sandoval and Torres exchanging breathtaking brass phrases with Jesús Rubalcaba underpinning on piano. García Caturla's rich, clear voice comes into its own in the swing of **U-LA-LA**, with Paquito D'Rivera on alto sax, Enrique Jorrín on violin and maestro Tata Güines on congas. She joins Miguelito Cuní and links the spicy percussion and brass on **Prepara Los Cueros**, with its highly funky tres and guitar offerings. The entrancing finale, **Maracaibo Oriental**, is an explosive dance fiesta.

Jan Fairley

Further listening: Hot Dance Music From Cuba, 1907–1936
(Harlequin/Interstate) **features many of the classic Cuban groups that fed both band members and inspiration into Las Estrellas.**

Fania All Stars

The Best Of Fania All Stars

Charly Schallplatten, 2000

Johnny Pacheco (flute, leader), Larry Harlow, "Papo" Lucca (piano), Luis "Perico" Ortiz (trumpet), Willie Colón (solo trombone), Yomo Toro (cuatro guitar), Bobby Valentín (bass), Ismael Miranda, Adalberto Santiago, Santos Colón, Hector Lavoe, Cheo Feliciano (vocals), Ray Barretto, Mongo Santamaría (congas), and others.

If one song by the Fania All Stars sums up the relationship between its stellar cast and its wildly enthusiastic audiences, it's Hector Lavoe's **Mi Gente**. The singer's Spanglish banter at the beginning is almost drowned out by the noise of the crowd, and it takes the full force of the brass section – a band in itself – and the thunderous Cuban percussion to quieten them. The greatest super-group in salsa history, FAS emerged in late-1960s New York in the wake of the Alegre and Tico All-Stars, who were experimenting with loosely structured descargas (jam sessions). In 1964, flautist Johnny Pacheco split to found a rival label – Fania – and signed up top-calibre musicians. Ten years on, Fania were performing at Yankee Stadium – a night preserved on several tracks of this two-CD compilation.

Fania was at the height of its popularity when these songs were recorded in the 1970s and 1980s. Arranger Larry Harlow was one of a clique (including trumpeter "Perico" Ortiz, vibes player Louie Ramirez, and pianist "Papo" Lucca) which had first created the "Sound of Salsa", and **Descarga Fania** and **Descarga En Cuba** are prime examples of their danceable improvisations. On the sensational eight-minute ensemble feast, **Por Eso Yo Toco La Salsa**, the top *salseros* reveal their characteristic vocal textures: Miranda's smooth rural tones, Santos

Colón rasping in the old Cuban style, velvety Cheo Feliciano, youthfully errant Rubén Blades, dignified Pete "El Conde" Rodríguez and – in an unforgivably rare appearance on this compilation – Celia Cruz, whose warm, assured contralto surpasses them all.

The traditional son and guajira styles all appear in big-band guise: **Tres Lindas Cubanas** has Johnny Pacheco's flute vying with Pupi Legaretta's Grapelli-influenced violin, while Cuban *guajiro* peasants are evoked in Ismael Miranda's **Soy Guajiro** (I Am a Peasant Farmer) – a strange choice for a man with gold jewellery and coiffed hair. Many of the band members were Puerto Rican, however, and the intense nine-minute workout, **Ponte Duro**, establishes a gently nationalist conga battle between Cuban Mongo Santamaría and NuYorican Ray Barretto (a draw). On the same track, Nicky Marrero's timbales thrash is awkwardly compulsive, while bongo player Roberto Roena, known as "El Gran Bailarín" (The Great Dancer), breaks off to dance, while perfectly maintaining his time-keeping cowbell ring. Roena reappears with husky Latin soul singer Ismael Rivera on **Bilongo Mandingo**, from 1981.

Fania All Stars were never an isolated group, as guests from jazz, rock and fusion testify. Cameroonian Manu Dibango appears with his global dance-floor hit, **Soul Makossa**, his biting sax cutting through the thick funk bass-lines. Electric guitarist Jorge Santana, leader of the Latin-rock band Malo, takes a restrained approach to Cheo Feliciano's anthem, **El Ratón**.

Breathtaking performances such as these explain the legendary reputation of the Fania All Stars. As each of the outstanding soloists also led their own band, it is hardly surprising that salsa's influence spread so far around the world, and endured for so long.

Sue Steward

Further listening: Richie Ray and Bobby Cruz's **Lo Mejor de Richie Ray and Bobby Cruz** (Vaya/Fania) brought a certain camp flair into mid-1970s New York salsa with Ray's florid and ebullient piano and Cruz's histrionic tenor vocals making a fabulous combination.

26

Cheo Feliciano

Salsa Caliente de NuYork!

Nascente, 2000

Cheo Feliciano (vocals), Larry Harlow (piano), Joe Cuba (congas, leader), Tommy Berrios (vibes), Nick Jiménez (piano), Jules "Slim" Codero (bass), Jimmy Sabater (timbales).

In salsa there is only one "Cheo", and for salsa fans of all ages, José "Cheo" Feliciano is an institution. Born in Puerto Rico, in 1938, his presence still sweetens political rallies and fills stadiums with salsa audiences at home in San Juan. His emotional shows always feature the ritual of adoring women thrusting red roses into his hands as he sings the ballads. He spends the rest of the show re-distributing them.

Cheo is a veteran of New York's 1960s boogaloo era, when he made his debut singing with Joe Cuba's Sextet, and several songs on this well-balanced compilation are those which established his reputation. Tailored to the youthful hybrid of Latin and Soul which erupted in New York, they also provide for the moment when salsa's dance aficionados settle down to smoochy Cuban boleros and salsa ballads. Cheo's popularity is based on his assured, professional, romantic performances, and particularly on his warm, elegant voice which moulds itself so distinctively to both upbeat and pensive moods – his careful pronunciation and vivid intonation greatly influenced the young Rubén Blades. In the 1970s and early 1980s, as New York salsa dominated the Latin world, Cheo toured and recorded with both the Fania All Stars and his own band, inspiring tremendous loyalty from his fans.

This selection covers an eighteen-year span, from the first hit,

El Ratón, from Joe Cuba's classic 1964 album, *Vagabundeando/Hanging Out*, to **Periódico de Siempre**, from Feliciano's hugely successful 1982 release, *Profundo*. "El Ratón" is a slowed-down, swaying boogaloo-ish charmer, Nick Jiménez's softly repeated piano riffs and Tommy Berrios's vibes lulling the listener along. The lyrics play with a triple-entendre about a cat-and-mouse game between *ratón* (boy/mouse) and *rata* (girl), throwing in references to drugs and Puerto Rican independence for good measure! "Periódico de Siempre", a spoof song about a newspaper, is a more complex period piece, awash with disco strings and featuring Mario Rivera's gritty, expletive baritone sax solo. The contrasting **Quinto Sabroso**, from 1964, is a racing Afro-Cuban frenzy, a showpiece for sparkling vibes and some spectacularly intricate timbales and cowbell rhythms. It's proof of conga-player Joe Cuba's flair for recreating a Cuban rumba on New York turf, and the young Feliciano has no difficulty keeping up with their fast-flowing melodies.

In **Salome**, a heart-rending salsa-ballad, Feliciano phrases across the bars against a teasing interplay of vibes and an exhilarating piano solo from Larry Harlow. The 1976 album, *Cheo*, yielded another evergreen, **Anacaona**, an uptempo homage to the hedonistic chief of an indigenous Caribbean tribe who is immortalized by her fondness for dancing and singing. A virtuoso range of harmonic and textural combinations back the vocals all through the compilation. A jazzy accompaniment to **Por Más Que Viva**, from 1987, makes for a fast, gritty effect. Flaring trumpets, grunting baritone sax and phased trombones work at a high pitch, pushing Feliciano into the high, urgent reaches favoured by Puerto Rican *salseros*. Closing the set, **Armonioso Cantar** moves in the direction of Cuban son with a novel combination of vibes and the mellowest cuatro guitar.

Sue Steward

Further listening: A 21-piece all-star team honours Puerto Rico's baseball hero on **Tributo Musical A Roberto Clemente** (Rykolatino). Classic New York son band, Conjunto Clásico, are led by "the Pavarotti of Salsa", Tito Nieves, on **Las Puertas Abiertas, Lo Mejor** (Vaya).

27

Ibrahim Ferrer

Buena Vista Social Club Presents Ibrahim Ferrer

World Circuit, 1999

Ibrahim Ferrer, Omara Portuondo, Pío Leyva, Teresa García Cartula, José Antonio
Rodríguez (vocals), Rubén González (piano), Ry Cooder (guitar), Manuel "Guajiro"
Mirabal (trumpet), Jesús "Aguaje" Ramos (trombone), Orlando "Cachaíto" López
(double bass), and others.

World Circuit, the independent record company who beat the American record industry Goliaths in the Grammy game with their album, *Buena Vista Social Club*, returned to Havana's EGREM studios a couple of years later with some of the same musicians, and more songs from the well-thumbed Cuban songbook. This time, the spotlight was on singer Ibrahim Ferrer, in an unashamedly romantic encounter with a previous era, filled with catchy, insistent melodies. The result – unless you have a heart of stone – is a magical, joyful experience.

Ferrer was already a favourite on the *BVSC* album, but after his appearance in Wim Wenders' affectionate documentary film, his popularity soared. In Cuba, he was remembered as the high-pitched, sweet-toned backing singer from Beny Moré's 21-piece band, but this first solo venture exposes the range and charms of his honeyed, soulful voice. Eleven mostly slow, romantic songs (bolero, son and a slow guajira) are bolstered by a couple of ravishing old-time dance numbers. Ferrer tackles Beny Moré's **Qué Bueno Baila Usted** at a fluid dancer's pace, for instance, with Amadito Valdés slapping out a mambo beat on timbales, Rubén Gonzalez playing a repetitive mambo piano groove, and

Cachaíto López whacking out thick, pivotal bass-lines as the saxes riff in choppy, mambo choruses and Jesús '"Aguaje" Ramos plays a muted trombone solo. Perfection.

Rubén Gonzalez relives his time with guitarist and songwriter Arsenio Rodríguez in the opening song, **Bruca Maniguá**, in which Ferrer interprets the potent lament of a slave escaping to the mountains in an emotive mix of African patois and Spanish. Rodríguez's **Mami Me Gustó** is a fast, flirty affair sung at a high, hoarse pitch, and measured in Armadito Valdés's thumping percussion and Cachaíto's lurching bass notes. It features solos from Papi Oviedo's shuffling tres guitar, González's effortlessly swinging, endlessly imaginative piano, and an explosive trumpet solo by Manuel "Guajiro" Mirabal. It epitomizes the musical richness and variety of the album.

A quartet of guitarists includes Ry Cooder, keeping rein on his rueful Hawaiian guitar, and Cuban country bluesmen Eliades Ochoa and "Papi'" Oviedo, but the texture of the album is dominated by Manuel Galbán's booming, tremolo-boosted guitar. On **Herido de Sombras**, the slowest of boleros (and a re-run of the 1960s hit by Galbán's pop group, Los Zafiros), a swirl of strings backs his spikey, dramatic guitar, as well as Ferrer's bitter-sweet vocals and the four-part harmony choruses by female vocalists, Gema 4. Of course, the record belongs to Ferrer's solo voice, and to his duets. On **Marieta** he is joined by Teresa García Cartula, but it is with Omara Portuondo that Ferrer really finds his perfect vocal match. Perhaps the most poignant moment in the *Buena Vista* film is when Ferrer and Portuondo sing the bolero **Silencio** face to face, and their contrasting voices enmesh just as beautifully off-camera. The album closes with Moré's bolero, **Como Fue** – "How it was, the day I fell in love" – a warming glimpse of Cuba's romantic heritage.

Sue Steward

**Further listening: Various Artists: Cuban Music Story –
Dance crazes from the Cuban Dynasty** (Rough Guides/World Music Network) "Cuba's musical history on a postcard"; on **Mayumbero** (Tumi Music), **Papi Oviedo** leads his own Cuban country band.

28

Fruko y Sus Tesos

Todos Bailan Salsa

World Music Network, 1998

Julio Ernesto Estrada Rincón, aka "Fruko" (bass, percussion, piano), Joe Arroyo, Wilson Manyomba Saoco, Willy Calderón (vocals), Issac Villanueva (composition), Enrique Henry Carillo (piano), Albertos Barros (trombone) and others.

When Colombia played in the 1998 World Cup, there was no debate about who would create the team song – Fruko, the Valderrama of Colombian salsa, had scored more hits with his productions than anyone in the country. **La Pachanga del Fútbol** was the magical result, with a Mexican wave of a chorus, verses describing soccer heroes Valderrama and Herrera in glorious action, and sampled chants of "Gollazooooooo!" from the home crowd. It's possibly the most infectious football anthem ever, and would have been a hit even if it had been endorsing the tinned tomatoes that earned the round-faced Rincón his nickname of "Fruko".

Fruko has provided the Colombian charts with hits since the early 1970s – when the undersized, under-aged teenager was first given control of the mixing desk at Discos Fuentes' studios in Medellín – and these eighteen tunes reveal the diversity of his releases. The still-sweet voice of the young Joe Arroyo is preserved in **Manyoma**, a typically agile affair whose words tumble on top of each other to the twisting upbeat rhythms of pianist Enrique Henry Carillo. Classic Fruko-Arroyo magic. Arroyo also sings his resonant composition, **Tania**, about leaving a girl behind in the country and heading for a new city life. Arroyo's co-vocalist from the 1970s, Saoco, sings Fruko's greatest hit, **El**

Preso (The Prisoner), a soulful salsa lament about life on death-row, delivered above a layer of trombones. Despite the theme, and Saoco's soulful voice, it preserves an upbeat optimism.

Arroyo and Saoco were the perfect vocal team – rough and smooth, agile and steady, unpredictable and reliable. Fruko himself is an exceptional all-rounder. As a young teenager, he played timbales on traditional cumbias and accordion-led vallenatos with Los Corraleros de Majagual, then switched to electric bass – his full, solid bass-lines thread through this compilation. Fruko employed a clique of inventive arrangers, led by Issac Villanueva and trombonist Alberto Barros, who is responsible for the profusion of trombone in Fruko's early records. Villanueva wrote **El Ausente**, an early hit for Arroyo, and this title song, **Todos Bailan Salsa** (Everyone's Dancing Salsa), which became an anthem throughout Latin America.

The collection includes some of Fruko's private passions, including instrumental re-makes of Pérez Prado's world-famous **Mambo No.5** and **Cereza Rosa**, the latter better known in English as "Cherry Pink and Apple-Blossom White". The tunes are as overblown as Prado's own versions, with braying brass and trumpet, guttural grunts and an electric guitar taking the place of Prado's piano. Fruko's (and Colombia's) passion for the jumpy pachanga rhythm, which had swept 1960s New York, is reflected in **Chachachá Con Pachanga** and **Swing Pachanga**, with timbales laying down the beat and spicing up the instrumental flavour.

Los Tesos were the prototype for Fruko's hit machine, a testing ground for later off-shoots such as the Latin Brothers and La Sonora Dinamita. Dancers found their rawness and passion irresistible, and they took Colombian salsa into the pan-Latin salsa charts for the first time, finally breaking the monopoly of New York and Puerto Rico.

Sue Steward

Further listening: The Latin Brothers' **Sobre Las Olas** (World Music Network) is engagingly rough and experimental, and reveals the best of Colombian salsa, with trilling piano and bouncy rhythms.

29

Carlos Gardel

The Best Of Carlos Gardel

EMI-Hemisphere, 1997

Carlos Gardel (vocals), Terig Tucci, Francisco Canaro, Alberto Castellanos (guitar), Vivas, Riverol, Barbieri, Pettorossi, Ricardo, Aguilar (conductors).

The ghost of Carlos Gardel, the Argentinian tango icon who died in a plane crash in 1935, still haunts the city he immortalized in the song **Mi Buenos Aires Querida** (My Beloved Buenos Aires). His most popular songs – cleaned and polished from the original 78rpm records for this collection – can still be heard in shopping malls, cafés and bars, and images of his gentle, lop-sided smile under a rakish fedora still adorn his beloved city. At the time of his death, aged 45, Gardel was a superstar throughout Latin America, and also adored in Paris and New York; his tragic demise fed the mythology of tango and built the Gardel legend.

Born in France, Gardel arrived at the age of three with his mother, who renamed Charles Gardes with the more Spanish-sounding Carlos Gardel. As a boy, he earned money singing folk songs in local bars and his special voice and charisma were soon acknowledged. In 1911, he launched a duo with the Uruguayan José Razzano, whose tenor was a perfect harmonic foil to Gardel's warbling baritone. But Gardel began to outshine his partner following the 1917 release of "Mi Noche Triste", and he went solo just as tango was spreading from the city's anarchic port-side haunts into more middle-class districts. His success was rapid and phenomenal, and he went on to export tango mania from Buenos Aires to Paris and beyond.

This compilation launches with **Mi Buenos Aires Querida**, recorded in 1934. "City of flowers", he sang, "When I see you again there'll be no more sorrow or forgetfulness", and the city fell at his feet. Gardel appeared in eight musical films in the 1930s, playing the kind of romantic Hollywood hero that Rudolf Valentino had established. **Cuesta Abajo**, the title track from Gardel's 1934 film, is a lament for lost love in which country boy loses girl to the city. **Tomo y Obligo** is quintessential tango fare: a self-pitying drinker broods over lost love while emptying a bottle, lulled by the choppy rhythms of the button accordion – the so-called "Voice of Tango", the bandoneón. In **El Día Que Me Quieras**, one of the most perfect of tangos, Gardel's impassioned plea glides over sustained violin chords, while in **Madreselva**, he darts around tantalizing pizzicato strings, bandoneón and piano. **Melodia de Arrabal** and **Leguisamo Solo** both return from string-laden orchestral backing to the simple format of acoustic guitars and entwined vocal harmonies, with no loss of emotional impact.

Gardel's songs (he co-wrote all but four of the twenty here) are unashamedly romantic but never cloying. Light relief comes with **Silencio**, in which he is joined by a wonderfully incongruous girlie chorus straight from an Esther Williams soundtrack, and **Rubias de Nueva York**, where the singer name-checks the blondes he's missing – "Peggy, Maggie, Betty and Julie" – to the sound of appropriately swelling strings. Gardel's melting baritone set the standard for every tango singer who followed, and earned him the nickname "Zorzal Azul" (Blue Thrush). His legend is undiminished; his tomb in Buenos Aires is still maintained by fans who strew flowers at the feet of his statue – and keep a cigarette burning in his hand.

Sue Steward

Further listening: The cracklier quality of **The Magic Of Carlos Gardel** (Harlequin/Interstate) perserves more of the atmosphere of the original 78s. **The Rough Guide to Tango** (World Music Network), a comprehensive compilation, includes Gardel's "Caminito", plus bandoneón magic from Anibal Troílo, Astor Piazzolla and Nestor Marconi.

30

Stan Getz and João Gilberto,
featuring Antonio Carlos Jobim

Getz/Gilberto

Verve, 1997

Stan Getz (tenor sax), João Gilberto (guitar, vocals), Antonio Carlos "Tom" Jobim (piano), Astrud Gilberto (vocals), Milton Banana (drums), Tommy Williams (bass).

In 1964, the Beatles were toppled from the US pop charts by a Brazilian single. Bossa nova, the "new way", had hit the world. Guitarist and singer João Gilberto went into a New York recording studio to make a bossa nova album with his partner, and bossa co-creator, Tom Jobim, and the jazz saxophonist Stan Getz, who had caught the bug a few years earlier. João's wife, Astrud, who used to sing her husband's songs at home, went along to translate. At some point during the sessions, Getz suggested that Astrud sing a couple of their songs – in English. On **The Girl from Ipanema**, which opens this fabulous memento of those recordings, Astrud joined João's lusciously cool, fruity Portuguese with her perfectly assured mellow tones and slightly off-kilter, sultry English – and seduced the world.

For the seven-inch version, also included here, João's original part was edited out and the song shot into the US charts, making Astrud an overnight star and earning her a Grammy. João, by contrast, only picked up his first Grammy in 2001, and was never half as well known internationally, though he is idolized in Brazil. "The Girl from Ipanema" became synonymous with Astrud's girlish cool and bossa nova's tropical languor and irresistible swing. Her untrained voice intuitively fits with João's awkward guitar melodies, and glides unselfconsciously across the softly choppy bossa rhythms that her husband created out of samba's wilder heritage. Her hits and misses with pitch just add to its seductiveness.

As "Ipanema" was to Astrud, so **Desafinado (Off Key)** belongs forever to João Gilberto. The title was a dig at critics who referred to the revolutionary bossa nova crowd as "off-key singers", but the converts recognized it as a brilliant collision of samba with American jazz. The guitar and vocal harmonies and gently syncopated rhythms were unlike anything before. In this perfect version, Stan Getz, a pioneer of America's West Coast "Cool Jazz", gets right inside the Brazilian rhythm and releases his melodies in controlled cascades of breathy exhalations. The tune defines bossa nova through the opposition of Jobim's tingly piano clusters and Gilberto's subtle vocal style and guitar chords, as Milton Banana measures the time in hissy hi-hat cymbal beats. **So Danço Samba**, written by the third member of the team that created bossa nova, lyricist Vinicius DeMoraes, is an untypically upbeat song about how Gilberto has had enough of twist, calypso and cha-cha-cha, and will only dance samba.

Getz adds an infectious "swing" whenever he breathes, and his full-on melodies cover whole bars, while the Brazilians operate on much more subdivided time-scales. The instrumental balance in these sessions is sometimes biased towards Getz, masking Gilberto's gentle, background chording and Jobim's spare, light-fingered technique. When Jobim does come to the fore – all too briefly – as on Astrud's **Corcovado**, it is magical. João's voice is at its best on **Para Machuchar Meu Coraçâo**, recorded so close to the microphone that it reveals its polished grain. It's as intimate as if he is singing into your ear while you sashay to the rhythms of his guitar. Utterly seductive.

Sue Steward

Further listening: The Legendary João Gilberto (Capitol/World Pacific) **is an exquisite private audience accompanied only by moodily offbeat guitar and light percussion. The Astrud Gilberto Album** (Verve, Silver Collection) **features bossified pop tailored to Astrud's sensual vocal style.**

Gilberto Gil

Unplugged

WEA, 1994

Gilberto Gil (vocals, violão, guitar), Arthur Maia (bass), Jorge Gomes (drums), Celso Fonseca (guitar), Marcos Suzana (percussion), Lucas Santana (flute).

Gilberto Gil's mellow, instantly recognizable voice and ear for a catchy tune have been at the heart of Brazilian pop for over thirty years. He is one of many leading Brazilian musicians from Salvador de Bahia, the unofficial capital of Afro-Brazil, and since he first became a major national star his music has reflected the eclecticism and complex rhythms of his native city. He is the perfect pop star and, together with Caetano Veloso, was the leading light of tropicalismo, that innovative blending of Brazilian rhythms and imagery with American rock which revolutionized Brazilian music in the late 1960s.

Gil was also one of the protagonists of a defining moment in Brazilian cultural history. On live television, at the height of the military dictatorship, in 1970, his close friend Caetano Veloso was booed by traditionalists during a song festival – which Gil won. Gil rushed onstage and draped his arm around his fellow cultural warrior while Veloso delivered an impassioned impromptu speech that became a manifesto for a generation. The military regime neither forgave nor forgot.

Gil and Veloso spent a couple of years in exile in London, only returning to Brazil as the political climate in the 1970s slowly improved. Gil settled into comfortable mega-stardom in the 1980s with a string of hits, but he seemed to have lost the bite that had made him a star in the first place. He spent extended periods in the Caribbean and was instrumental in introducing reggae to Brazil, but a new generation of hungrier, more innovative Bahian musicians, like Carlinhos Brown, were looking more to Africa for their influences. As they began to transform Salvador's carnival into the most musically influential in Brazil, Gil's reggae-pop seemed increasingly lightweight in comparison. A couple of years as Salvador's Municipal Secretary of Culture merely underlined his drift towards the middle of the road.

A dramatic return to form came in 1992, first with a superb album recorded with Veloso, *Tropicalismo 2*, and then with a couple of fine solo albums, *Parabolicamara*, in 1994, and *O Sol de Oslo*, four years later. This collection, recorded live for Brazilian MTV's *Unplugged* series, comes from the middle of this renaissance period, and includes tracks from every stage of his career. **Parabolicamara** is the title track of his recent comeback album, while **Sampa**, a classic love song to the city of São Paulo, written by Veloso, was covered on his first album, in 1968. Several other songs – such as **Aquele Abraço**, Gil's love song to Rio de Janeiro, and **Expresso 2222**, an uptempo dance number about a backlands train – are as well known to Brazilians as Beatles standards in the English-speaking world.

But it is a couple of the lesser-known tracks that show Gil's talent at its best. **Tenho Sede** blends the harsh imagery and melodic, yearning rhythms of the northeastern interior, while **A Paz** is a subtle, quiet semi-bossa, brilliantly sung. And there is also the original version of **Toda Menina Baiana**, a hit on London's late-1980s club scene, but which was originally recorded by Gil in the early 1970s. It is sung here by the master returning to the top of his form.

David Cleary

Further listening: Tropicalismo 2 (WEA) is a brilliant 1992 revisiting of tropicalismo by its founding fathers, Veloso and Gil. On Gil's Grammy-winning **Quanta – Ao Vivo** (Mesa), the lyrical themes are a leap away from the usual samba subjects. Djavan's love songs have been covered by Gil, Costa, Veloso and others; **Djavan** (Columbia) is probably his best – buy the Brazilian-language version.

Celina González

Santa Bárbara

EGREM, 1993

No musicians credited.

Celina González is the Queen of Cuban Country Music – as she states in the opening song of this album, "*Yo soy el punto cubano*" (I *am* Cuban country song). Celina stayed in Cuba when so many of her musical contemporaries fled to the US, so her music took longer to spread to the wider world than that of singers like Celia Cruz. But today, towards the end of her career, she is adored all through Latin America and in many pockets of Europe.

For years, she recorded a daily radio show of country music, her *guajira* (peasant) radio "family" playing everyday songs about country life while she sang. Her first broadcast, in Havana in 1948, was a duet with her husband, the singer-guitarist Reutilio Domínguez, as "Celina y Reutilio"; that duo is recalled here on **El Encanto De Tu Boca**, now with brisk trumpet and tres guitar supporting the beautifully interwoven harmonies. Celina has re-recorded their hits over and over in different formats ever since. In the recording studio, she sang note-and-pitch perfect; first time, no retakes. Her pure, high and occasionally deliberately tremulous voice would silence the room.

With her long frilly skirts and embroidered blouses, her high-heeled mules and make-up, and the red flower in her hair, Celina González was *the* lipstick revolutionary. An unambiguously committed socialist, she lived an urban life in Havana, far removed from the childhood spent in the sugar plantation state of

Matanzas. But she inherited her family's Spanish looks, their guitar-based guajira songs and their ten-line poems called *décimas* and at the same time was also submerged in the African heritage of neighbouring states; it is these twin elements that work her emotive Cuban alchemy.

The first song Celina wrote, around 1948, was **A Santa Bárbara**, an Afro-Cuban hymn to the warrior god Chango, St Barbara's counterpart in the *santería* cult. She has re-recorded it countless times, and it has continued to be her signature tune long after Reutilio's death (in 1971). This version has a modern, funky arrangement, as she enters through a blustering trombone, her refined voice rising from its midst like rich incense smoke. Other songs are (literally) more down to earth: odes to the Cuban landscape and the people living there. **Paisajes Naturales** is an unrestrained tribute to Cuba's "lovely palms and skies". She also evokes the rum-stoked musical parties (*guateques*) outside thatched huts (*bohíos*) under the stars, in **Guateque Campesino** and **Guateque de Mi Bohío**, songs that brought solace to generations of city-locked country people like herself. She uses that slight vibrato effect to enhance the sentiment, and is accompanied by a delicately picked tres guitar and soft, muted vibraphone. She retained the vibes in her band longer than most commercial guajira singers, and it reappears on **Aguacero, Aguacero**, a story of a day in the country.

Taking a brisker, horse-cantering pace, the album's son tunes introduce the characteristic trumpet solos (in league with trombone and tres guitar) to great effect in the magical **Mi Son Es Un Misterio** and **No Mixtifiques Mi Son** and **Mi Reto**. But the album's most distinctive number, **Aurora**, is a bolero with the wonderfully decadent air of 1930s Paris. Celina's tone is quite transformed – and she seems to relish the change.

Sue Steward

Further listening: La Rica Cosecha (TUMI Music) is backed by a more rootsy band. The essential Celina González album, **Fiesta Guajira** (World Circuit) is deleted, so seek it out in second-hand shops: it features most of the same great songs, but backed by her original radio band.

33

Rubén González

Chanchullo

World Circuit, 2000

Rubén González (piano), Ibrahim Ferrer, Cheikh Lô (vocals), Manuel "Guajiro" Mirabal (trumpet), Jesús "Aguaje" Ramos (trombone), Richard Egües (flute), Ry Cooder, Eliades Ochoa, Papi Oviedo (guitar), "Cachaíto" López (bass), and others.

This record marks a late chapter in the fairy-tale story of Cuban pianist Rubén González. In 1996 he languished at home with arthritically crippled hands and a piano destroyed by wood-worm, wondering whether a friend's prophecy that he would achieve fame late in life would come to pass. Within a year, his chance playing on the *Buena Vista Social Club* and *Afro-Cuban All Stars* albums brought the answer, and he and fellow musicians were flying between the choicest concert halls of Europe. Most important, González was playing piano almost every day. And how! Playing seemed to quell the arthritis and, after five years' absence, his hands unfurled, becoming a conduit for the stored-up melodies and rhythms of a century of Cuban popular music. His effortless improvisations drive, lead or punctuate all the tunes on this album.

Rubén González's first solo album, *Introducing Rubén González*, was an unplanned spin-off from the *BVSC* sessions, rightly praised and heavily purchased. **Chanchullo**, the follow-up, was carefully planned, and reveals the musical benefits of the pianist's new life and the stimulating effect of his intense new musical interactions. Tunes ebb and flow organically, and – to paraphrase the title of the wonderful cha-cha-cha, **Rico Vacilón** – swing like crazy. (This wonderfully upbeat tune is one of Ry Cooder's few prominent moments, with a jangling blues guitar solo; he otherwise stays in the shadow of Eliades Ochoa's robust country guitar and Papi Oviedo's emotive tres.)

This is group work by a bunch of endlessly imaginative soloists. Their improvising brilliance can be best heard on the descargas (structured jam sessions) which open and close the record – **Chanchullo** and the energizing, piano-led **Pa' Gozar** – as well as on **La Lluvia**, a genuinely impromptu reaction to the studio's leaking roof, driven by a clacking clave beat that sounds just like rain on tin.

"Chanchullo" is based on Israel "Cachao" López's original "Mambo", which laid the trail to the world's 1950s dance craze. It opens to chunky, pounding piano chords playing a syncopated mambo beat and distills down to González's extraordinary, impressionistic solo. Cachao's nephew, Cachaíto, works close to Rubén's piano, the two men picking up on rhythms concealed in the tunes at an almost psychic level. Cachao's **Isora Club** is performed here at a traditionally sedate pace which tests the skill of Jesús "Aguaje" Ramos's trombone. Aguaje and trumpeter Manuel "Guajiro" Mirabal, reappear in the sensational, swinging **El Bodeguero**, a smash hit for Cuba's leading cha-cha-cha band, Orquesta Aragón, whose former flautist, Richard Egües, steals the spotlight with a long, trilling, searing, solo.

Arsenio Rodríguez, González's mentor, is paid tribute on **De Una Manera Espantosa**, sung by Ibrahim Ferrer in a gloriously husky style in front of a hot brass front-line. That brassy, big-band Rodríguez son formula is repeated on **Choco's Guajira**, on which Ferrer is joined by Senegal's Cheikh Lô. Each song is a highly sophisticated group experience, but shining through every one, like sunshine through trees, is piano solo after solo by the re-awoken Rubén González.

Sue Steward

Further listening: Introducing Rubén González (World Circuit) was knocked off in two days after the Buena Vista recording had officially finished. **Afro-Cuban All Stars** (World Circuit), the companion piece to Buena Vista, includes some brilliant solos from González.

34

El Gran Combo de Puerto Rico

Nuestra Música

Combo Records, 1985

Rafael Ithier (piano), Charlie Aponte, Jerry Rivas, Papo Rosario (vocals), Taty Maldonado, Víctor "El Cano" Rodríguez (trumpet), Eddie Pérez, Freddie Miranda (alto sax), Fanny Ceballos (trombone), Fernando Pérez (bass), Edgardo Morales (timbales), José Miguel "Michel" Laboy (bongos), Miguel Torres (conga),

True *salseros* — keepers of the faith that takes its communion on dance floors, devotees of the *clave* rhythm that governs salsa — believe that El Gran Combo de Puerto Rico may just possibly be the world's greatest dance band. Even among the less fervently religious, few will quibble that this peerless group has ever delivered anything other than a sensational set of irresistible infectiousness. And nobody, anywhere in the world, can stand still when they play the hits from nearly forty years of best-selling albums. El Gran Combo are still rolling out their discs with metronomic accuracy of taste, style and swing. How extraordinary, then, that a Christmas album should be thought of as their finest release…

The verve of El Gran Combo precisely reflects the hard-won ascendancy of Puerto Rican salsa in the 1980s, when all the nonsense about "stealing" Cuban music and not comparing with the sophisticated crossover styles of New York salsa was brushed aside by a dozen of the island's bands that suddenly achieved thrilling maturity. El Gran Combo, indisputable musical kings of the island since 1962, were first among equals, and **Nuestra Música** (Our Music) is a celebration of Puerto Rico's newfound musical confidence, showing a fierce dedication to the listening and dancing needs of fellow Boricuas (Puerto Ricans). Every track is an unashamedly uplifting dance number, unerringly concocted to fuel the rounds of parties that are essential during Puerto Rico's Christmas season.

The opening song, **La Fiesta de Pilito**, complains about the problems of last year, adding that maybe there's worse to come but at least there's January round the corner and Christmas to celebrate in the meantime. "Let's go to Pilito's, everyone – *todo Puerto Rico-o-o* – to eat cakes, suckling pig, rice'n'peas, black pudding. You name it, let's have it!" All the excitability and enthusiasm of the revellers is put across not just with shouting and cheering, but with a tune and arrangement that pins your ears back and propels you ruthlessly to the dance floor.

There's barely time to draw breath before EGC launches into another party number, a fantasy of name-checking a spiralling list of salsa guests. More and more luminaries arrive until Celia Cruz shouts out "*No hay cama pa' tanta gente!*" – "There's no beds to put up all these people!" More whooping and shouting accompany another typically joyful, attacking EGC tune.

Leader and pianist Rafael Ithier's arrangements are unmistakable: trumpets and sax play big block chords, leaving a sole trombone for ballast. The commitment is always to dance, leaving little room for such self-indulgence as soloing. The album's pace is unrelenting, but two numbers vary the festive theme with a rallying cry to the people of Puerto Rico not to lose their identity by forgetting their traditions. **Cosas Del Campo** refers to the country customs that just "feel right", while the most moving song – and not merely pelvically – is a funny, warm tribute to **El Jíbaro Listo**, the "Shrewd Peasant" who finds success in the city.

Tommy Garcia

Further listening: El Combo de Siempre (JeSiKa Records) features a brilliant group of EGC alumni. **Bailando Con El Mundo 30 Aniversario** (Combo Records) gives an excellent insight into El Gran Combo's achievement, with a glorious hit for every triumphant year as far as 1992. But it might be worth waiting for 2002, and the definitive forty-year feast.

35

Grupo Niche

Me Huele A Matrimonio

Codiscos, 1986

Jairo Varela (composer, vocals), Tito Gómez (vocals), Francisco García (bass), Nicolás "Pichirilo" Cristancho (piano), Ostwal Serna (tres guitar), Myke Potas (congas), Alfredo "Pichirilo" Longa (timbales), Jairo Riascos (bongos), and others.

Colombia needs no help to promote its image of illegality. The bitter truth about Jairo Varela, leader of Grupo Niche during its most impeccable first incarnation, is that though undeniably a great musician, his fame and achievements have been overshadowed by his notoriety and incarcerations. His background of poverty and lack of education make him typical of his nation, but his ability to overcome musical illiteracy to create one of the most important salsa bands of the 1980s, Grupo Niche, is an extraordinary achievement.

Varela's original collaborator, the gifted trombonist and arranger Alexis Lozano, tells of how he was introduced to the recently released Varela on the street in Bogotá, Varela was armed with an apparently never-ending supply of songs, and knew exactly how he wanted the band to sound, but he needed the literate Lozano (and later, subsequent replacements) to transcribe the melodies and harmonies. They returned to Cali, the only region in Colombia with a tradition of salsa, and set about recording an album.

The jawsocking impact of Niche's first release, *Querer Es Poder*, was due to its swing. Varela understood exactly how a great salsa number works, and introduced ideas such as the use of the sax and flute to offset the standard trumpet-trombone combination.

The band had a youthful urgency and attack that presaged greatness. A telling feature of the Niche sound was the trombones played by brothers Alberto and Adolfo Barros, who went on to form Los Titanes and make a couple of ingeniously executed romantic salsa albums. While with Grupo Niche, Adolfo was also involved in transcribing the maestro's musical ideas.

Me Huele A Matrimonio (This Smells Of Marriage To Me – a dry dig at musicians' terror of commitment) is the culmination of the original Niche sound. It introduces the veteran Puerto Rican singer, Tito Gómez, whose melancholic voice is what Varela must always have wished his own poorer instrument had sounded like. The choice of Gómez as lead vocalist was brilliantly judged, and sealed Niche's identity. Then, in a very public row over money, almost the entire original band left Varela. They went on to form a band called Los Niches but, lacking Varela's motivating spirit, the new venture quickly foundered. *Matrimonio* is a marvellous testament to the music they had created with Varela before the split.

Three songs in particular, **Un Caso Social**, **Ese Día** and **Para Mi Negra Un Son** were enormous hits, and stand out as among Varela's best work. They are always featured in any compilation, powered along by sharp, sometimes haunting lyrics, that Gómez voice and the thumping, driving swing that is Varela's own. The wit and insouciance of **Me Huele A Matrimonio** and **La Trampa** are seductive, while the instrumental-with-chorus, **La Rata Chillona**, is a crisp jam featuring a pounding piano solo by Nicolás Cristancho.

The snazzy record sleeves sees a cartoon Varela steppin' out as a check-suited, spat-booted player, a million miles from matrimony. There are no clichés of the tropical sweat'n'buttock record-sleeve variety here.

Tommy Garcia

Further listening: Apriétala (Codiscos), by Los Titanes – the group founded by ex-Niche trombonists Albert and Adolfo Barros – is a swinging disc of late-1980s Colombian salsa. **Internacional** (Codiscos) is the album of choice from Grupo Gale, a modern Colombian salsa band.

36

Juan Luis Guerra & 4.40

Bachata Rosa

Kâreń, 1990

Juan Luis Guerra, Roger Zayas Bayán, Adalgisa Pantaleón, Marco Hernández
(vocals), Armando Beltre (trumpet), Daniel Peña (sax), Roberto Olea (trombone),
Gonzalo Rubalcaba (piano), and others.

Play a track from the explosive
Bachata Rosa (Pink Bachata) on
any dance floor and watch everyone jump on it. Juan Luis Guerra
and 4.40 released their masterpiece back in 1990, and it quickly
became a phenomenon, selling
over five million copies. The
album's success took the genial,
lanky Guerra straight to the top,
and placed the Dominican
Republic's bachata and merengue dance styles – both once
derided as low-class – firmly on the musical map.

Guerra's magic came from approaching his country's rural folk
forms with the mind of a musician trained in composition and
jazz. He has an eclectic contemporary appetite, drawing on
influences as diverse as the Beatles and the singer-songwriters of
nueva canción, as well as the great range of Cuban, Caribbean,
Central and North American salsa music – not to mention his
studious interest in Dominican folk. 4.40 created a smooth,
modern sound by keeping the guitars of the original rustic format but replacing the accordion, scraper and bass marimba with
flowing synthesized sounds.

The album develops a single theme of the overwhelming
nature of falling in love, and the joyous mood is established by
Rosalía, suffused with the wordy, teasing pleasures of impatient
desire. Blasts of horn riffs impudently herald and then frisk

around 4.40's hallmark choruses, playing off against Guerra's strikingly nasal *salsero* tones. On the smoochily slow bachata, **Como Abeja Al Panal** (Like A Bee To The Bee Hive), Guerra duets with Adalgisa Pantaleón, playing out a proposal of marriage from an over-eager suitor to a girl dithering in allegiance.

The jazzy salsa piano of Cuban Gonzalo Rubalcaba, which ranges through the disc, opens the upbeat **Carta de Amor**, which describes the way obsessive love excludes everything else. The musical traditions of the Dominican Republic's African and indigenous populations can be heard in the Afro-Indian chanted chorus that leads into *Bachata Rosa's* glorious centrepiece, **A Pedir Su Mano** (Asking You To Marry Me), whose syncopating rhythms hint at sexual frisson. Images of a country wedding are evoked by flashes of brass over swinging keyboard rhythms. The song's pre-nuptial anticipation culminates in the fever of **La Bilirrubina**, whose infectious rhythms underscore the conclusion that the only cure can be insulin shots of love.

The tenderly erotic **Burbujas de Amor** (Love Bubbles), with its guitar-percussion dynamic, conjures up the physical aura of love-making, Guerra aching to become a fish able to rub his nose in his lover's fish-tank. **Bachata Rosa** itself, with its quoted lines from love poems by Chilean Nobel prize winner, Pablo Neruda, is imbued with post-coital bliss, symbolized by a rose, and by Guerra's own nonchalant whistling as he walks away into tropical rain. This leads neatly to **Reforéstame**, when Adalgisa Pantaleón's soaringly clear voice likens the growth of love to nature's nourishment of plants.

The ricocheting merengue which closes the album, **Acompáñeme Civil**, is a surprise. Quite unexpectedly, Guerra tells a dark story of police corruption, prefiguring his political stance on subsequent releases.

Jan Fairley

Further listening: Guerra's follow-up album, **Areito** (BMG) developed his modernizing of traditional genres. **The Rough Guide to Merengue and Bachata** (World Music Network) runs from traditional, accordion-led styles to those influenced by reggae and hip-hop.

37

Alfredo Gutiérrez y su Conjunto

Lo Mejor de Alfredo Gutiérrez y su Conjunto

MTM/Columbia, 1998

Alfredo Gutiérrez (accordion, vocals, leader), Hermán de Lavalle, Dino Gutiérrez (bass), Harold Lengua (guitar), Ramón Bertel (guacharaca), and others

Of the myriad folk styles played across Colombia, it is cumbia and vallenato that have become national and international favourites, and potent reminders of home for millions of Colombians living abroad. Vallenato's home territory is the coastal northeast of Colombia, near the Venezuelan border, centred on the dusty, cowboy town of Valledupar – known as "the cradle of vallenato". Valledupar put itself on the map in 1968, with the first Festival of Vallenato, and every April now sees a vallenato frenzy as hundreds of accordionists compete for the title of Vallenato King. In 1969, the young Alfredo Gutiérrez, from nearby Sucre province, won this coveted award. He repeated the trick twice more in the 1980s, and today, he is *the* king.

The original vallenato groups were trios featuring a button accordion, a small, conical, high-pitched drum (the caja) and the instrument that adds the itch, the guacharaca, a güiro-like scraper made of bamboo. Other instruments have gradually been introduced, including Spanish guitar, the gaita (a bamboo flute associated with cumbia) and inevitably, in the 1970s, electric guitars and bass, which became the essential source of the characteristic 2/4 hopping beat. By the 1980s, modern electric vallenato groups also featured congas, cowbells and timbales – and closely resembled salsa bands, but for the accordion. On this album, Gutiérrez also includes trombone, trumpet, clarinet and French horn.

As a fifteen-year-old, in 1961, Gutiérrez joined pioneering big band, Los Corraleros de Majagual, and within a couple of years, he was playing accordion solos and singing his own songs. When he eventually formed his own band, it caused a sensation. A born showman, Gutiérrez even plays his accordion with his toes, or holds it behind his head. But nothing detracts from his phenomenal technique. He can draw from the instrument every shade of emotion: never saccharine, often sweet; light-fingered and punchy; pouring careening melodies and screeching cries or soulful sweet tunes; and simulating the catches and ululations of his own high, sweet and endlessly flexible voice.

These 24 original greatest hits operate in matching pairs, segueing into each other. **Dos Mujeres**, a jokey discussion about having two love affairs, moves at a slow, seductive pace evoking swaying skirts and hips, then shifts into **Fiesta En Guarare**, whose lyrics are – like most vallenato's – mundane and repetitive ("We're going, my love, to the festival at Guarare"). The hissy guacharaca controls the beat and the accordion's sustained notes hang, provocatively, then plunge with all the drama of an Olympic acrobat. An agile trombone mimics his accordion lines as he soars into throbbing yodels that melt the heart.

In **Dime Que Por Qué**, Gutiérrez's style evokes the haunting melancholy of tango's bandoneón. Soft, delicate notes engage with a fragile acoustic guitar, and occasionally break into heart-rending sighs. Harp-like keyboards accompany the accordion on **Paloma Guaramera**, a song about a dove flying back to the countryside from the town. Gutiérrez adopts the highest falsetto to represent the dove's joy at flying over fields again. The thrice-crowned king, forty years in the business, is quite able to crush his instrument's tendency to melancholy – and, with plenty of volume, to pump joy deep into the soul.

Sue Steward

Further listening: Los Corraleros de Majagual's **14 Éxitos** (Discos Fuentes) showcases the veteran cumbia and vallenato big band. Husky voiced Lisandro Meza is second only to Gutiérrez: try **Cumbia** (World Circuit).

38

India

Lo Mejor de India

MCA/RMM, 1996

India (vocals), Marc Anthony (vocals), Eddie Palmieri (piano), Charlie Sepúlveda (trumpet), Sergio George (producer), and others.

Forget Christina Aguilera, the *Latinas* whose faces fill the Hispanic music magazines and whose shows sell out all over the continent have yet to impinge on the wider world. In the mid 1990s, two young NuYoricans, India and Marc Anthony, swept into the charts alongside the salsa greats.

Linda "La India" Caballero and Marc Anthony Muñiz, both born in 1969, took a long route into salsa: Marc Anthony learnt to sing and play guitar with his father, a folk singer; India took opera classes. Their teens coincided with Latin New York's electro-dance music, known as freestyle, and while most singers mimed to backing tapes, these two sang live. India was a soul-girl. Her first solo record, *Dancing in the Fire* (1986), was a belting collision of hip-hop and soul, with little trace of salsa. Marc Anthony's debut, *When the night is over* (1990), was similarly more hip-hop than salsa, but included prestigious solos by Tito Puente, salsa trumpeter Luis "Perico" Ortiz, and pianist Eddie Palmieri; not bad for a 21-year old.

Vivir Lo Nuestro, a live recording of which opens this 1996 greatest-hits compilation, is a memento of the two singers' early closeness and a classic soul-salsa love duet. It reveals their quite different vocal personalities: Marc Anthony's mature and expansive delivery is offset by India's more free-style operatic contralto. The backing is quintessential Sergio George – a key producer of the era – with thick funk bass-lines, modulated trombone choruses and sharp trumpets softened by his sweet electric piano.

In 1993, on the arm of Eddie Palmieri, India recorded the marvellously infectious club hit, a six-minute boogaloo-salsa, **Llegó La India** (Here Comes India). Singing in English and Spanish, she handles the fast twisting rhythms of this passionate ode to New York; Palmieri plays a lengthy piano solo, typically dense and clever, and Charlie Sepúlveda drops in a searing trumpet solo. It is easily the high point of the album.

Sniffy elders had to take note as the enfants terribles hit the charts, often appearing on the same bills, and brought in droves of new young fans. India's voice still had a hit-and-miss quality, but her instinct and her energy, combined with the imaginative support of the top-grade RMM musicians, created something delightful. Virtuosity was no longer critical, and instead of forming part of an organic salsa orchestra, these singers were more like solo rock stars.

Performing live with Celia Cruz, India prostrated herself before singing a duet of Palmieri's **Yemaya y Ochún**. In the solo version on this album, India's voice is charmingly girlish – somewhat reminiscent of the young La Lupe, though far less intuitively wild – but she handles the challenging cross rhythms provided by the Afro-Cuban percussion robustly. Eddie Palmieri's **Mi Primera Rumba** is a brave choice, considering that rumba singers are the most skilled of Afro-Cuban singers, treasured for their rhythmic dexterity and improvised solos. India is not an improviser, but she makes the song hers – with the assistance of Sergio George's trombone-laden orchestra. This record is as much a showcase of his late 1980s/early 1990s sound as of India's vocals. The choice salsa-ballad **Nunca Voya Olvidarte** includes his trademark use of stuttering trumpet choruses, inspired by Cuba's hot new sound, timba.

Sue Steward

Further listening: Foremost among the 1990s torrent of Latina singers was the startlingly original Puerto Rican Olga Tañón, whose live album, **Olga Viva, Viva Olga** (WEA), shows off her perfected merengue style. Marc Anthony's **Contra la Corriente** (RMM) shot him into the salsa history books.

39

Inti-Illimani

The Best Of Inti-Illimani

Xenophile Green Linnet Records, 2000

Horacio Salinas (guitar, vocals, leader), Horacio Durán (charango), Jorge Coulón
(guitar, harp), Marcelo Coulón (guitar, percussion), José Seves (guitar, vocals, box),
Efrén Viera (clarinet, percussion), Jorge Ball (flute, vocals), and others.

Following Pinochet's bloody military coup in 1973, Chilean group
Inti-Illimani used to joke that
they were on the longest tour in
history. They had found themselves stranded in Europe, and fifteen years of exile followed. It
was hardly wasted time. An early,
student passion for Andean music
and instruments transformed into
a full career, and the band became
the heart and soul of the international solidarity movement. Inti-
Illimani challenged Pinochet with their energy, inventiveness and
engagement. They represented the nueva canción (New Song)
generation that reclaimed Latin American music, and practically
reinvented the Andean sound.

This compilation focuses on the group's last four discs, all produced since their return to Chile in 1988. It kicks off with
Angelo, which sounds traditionally Andean but is in fact a composition by musical director Horacio Salinas. He uses a characteristic interplay of acoustic strings, embroidering the melody
with quena bamboo flutes. **Kulliacas** – which reworks a 1960s
piece, "Recuerdos de Kalahuayo", with a delightful, panpipe-led
Peruvian melody – and **Yamor** – a lively Ecuadorian dance for
the Festival of San Juanito – are in a similar vein, but boosted by
the addition of Latin percussion. **Arpa Peruana** and **Entre
Amor** are both intimate performances showcasing solo instru-

ments; the latter features the gently bewitching virtuoso Horacio Durán playing the indigenous charango guitar, accompanied by an accordion's tango touches.

Inti-Illimani's most impressive and vibrant work has emerged from their close collaborations with iconoclastic Chilean singer-songwriter, Patricio Manns. After an immensely hard, but musically fertile, exile in Italy, the album *Amar de Nuevo* (Falling In Love Again), was the first disc they made after being allowed back to Chile. It is represented here by the flirtatious **La Fiesta Eres Tú** which, in common with the rest of the album, re-invents the 1950s Creole romantic serenades. **Antes de Amar de Nuevo** is quintessential nueva canción, with a chirpy sax and violin playing a waltz while the lyrics fuse falling in love with the notion of returning home to fall in love – again – with Chile. "Before falling in love again, cry a little in silence, be as the rain washing the window, the sun is not far away ... to see it you only have to open the morning".

Most Inti-Illimani vocal arrangements – such as the mischievous **Mulata**, which uses a wonderfully rhythmic poem by Black Cuban Nicolás Guillén, and the Puerto Rican salsa classic, **El Negro Bembón** – typically intermingle one, two, three voices then chorus, like an intricate doowop group. Star moments of the compilation are the dance-song, **Negra Presuntuosa**, and the Peruvian classic, **Fina Estampa**, which features the gloriously seductive vibrato of José Seves and the wonderful rhythms of the percussion box.

The Andean song-dance **Salake**, which closes the collection, evokes the original inspiration for the band which first came together, as a group of poncho-clad students, to play the continent's pre-Colombian music. They imitate an Andean village band, with pan-pipers approaching from a distance as the singing finally fades back into the South American landscape.

Jan Fairley

Further listening: Fellow nueva canción groups Quilapayún and Illapu feature on **The Music Of the Andes** (EMI-Hemisphere), while **The Rough Guide to the Music of the Andes** (World Music Network) offers Inti-Illimani, Victor Jara and a mix of Bolivian and Peruvian contemporaries.

40

Irakere

Bailando Así

EGREM/Fonomusico, 1986

Chucho Valdés (piano, keyboards, leader), José Luis Cortes (flute, sax), Oscar Valdés (vocals, batá drums, percussion), Enrique Pla (drums), Carlos Emilio Morales (guitar), Carlos del Puerto (bass), Jorge Varona (trumpet), Juan Munguia (trombone), and others.

Irakere is one of the most significant bands to emerge from post-revolutionary Cuba, an outrageously inventive organization founded by pianist Chucho Valdés in 1973. The name derives from the Yoruba word for that part of the forest where drummers gather. In the mid 1980s, when this disc was made, Irakere were cultural ambassadors for Cuban music, which was still cocooned by the embargo. Residencies at Ronnie Scott's Jazz Club in London contributed to the booming interest in Latin music in Europe, but it was always inaccurate to limit Irakere to "Latin jazz" – as Ronnie Scott's Club discovered when they were forced to remove tables and allow dancing.

Bailando Así (Dancing Like This) represents the band's second phase, after saxophonist Paquito D'Rivera and trumpeter Arturo Sandoval had defected to the US. Valdés hired the young flautist and composer from Los Van Van, José Luis Cortés, who easily filled the void. His **Rucu Rucu A Santa Clara**, named after a dance rhythm, is quintessential late-1980s Irakere – helplessly danceable, as joyful as carnival music (the choruses have a samba flavour) and built on a marvellously intricate weave of ensemble playing and inventive solos. Chucho's opening piano melody lays a trail for the brass: Cortés's snorting baritone saxophone playing against the shrill trumpet. Singer Oscar Valdés is a natural improviser, reared on Afro-Cuban religious chants.

Chucho led Irakere from the piano, maintaining a seamless flow of music and solos that reflect an eclectic and encyclopaedic knowledge of Cuban music, the Western classical tradition and jazz. **Boliviana**, a gorgeous bolero-son dedicated to a young Bolivian woman, sees Cortes adopting the tone of Andean pan-pipes and playing long, trilling, bird-songs. Electric bassist, Carlos del Puerto, plays melodies as well as the repetitive rhythm patterns which anchor salsa. **Bailando Así** shifts from a delicate piano intro into an abandoned dance track. Chucho drops in a familiar salsa refrain on his newly purchased electric keyboards and the band release a series of joyful upbeat solos.

Homenaje a Beny Moré connects Irakere with the iconic Moré, whose orchestra reshaped intelligent dance music in the 1950s. Moré's great hit, "Que Buena Baila Usted" (How well you dance) is paraphrased as "Que banda tiene usted" (What a band you've got), and is a magnificent dance number, powered with stonking saxophones (including Cortes's cavorting baritone) and awhirl with Chucho's joyful melodies. Oscar Valdés possesses none of Moré's lyricism but his rough-edged voice has its own appeal. The stop-start, jerky rhythms were quite shocking after the reassuring smoothness of the salsa romantica that then domi-nated the Latin charts.

Irakere became a finishing school for some of the greatest soloists and inventors in Cuban dance music. In 1988 Cortés took off with half the band and founded the pioneering NG La Banda, which now leads the new wave of Cuban timba salsa, while Chucho Valdés works increasingly on solo projects abroad. This record, then, is a precious momento of an era, a timelessly brilliant collection by one of the most important bands in Latin music.

Sue Steward

Further listening: The Best of Irakere (Columbia/Sony) is a re-issue of the sensational 1978 Grammy winner, headed by the original trio of Valdés, D'Rivera and Sandoval. **Cuban Jazz – 90 miles to Cuba** (RMM/Tropijaz) reunites Chucho and his father, Bebo Valdés.

41

Víctor Jara

Complete

Pläne (Germany), 1993

Víctor Jara (guitar, vocals).

Víctor Jara has become famous as the Chilean singer murdered by the brutal Pinochet regime in September 1973, and Peter Gabriel and Sting are just two artists who have taken his name to audiences worldwide. But while many know his dramatic story, few have heard him sing; this four-CD box set of his complete works is one of the few discs available outside Chile. It is glorious from start to finish.

Jara was born into a rural family. His father worked the land until his death, whereupon the family moved to a shanty town in the Chilean capital, Santiago. His mother was a popular local singer and Jara's innate knowledge of folk music came directly from her. His intelligence and talent – in the absence of conventional qualifications – earned him a place at Santiago Theatre School and the rest, as they say, is history. He was one of the founding group of singers invited by Ángel and Isabel Parra as regulars at their nightclub, the Peña de los Parra, which became a key meeting place during the short years of Salvador Allende's Marxist government.

The majority of songs in this set feature simply Jara and his acoustic guitar, strumming folk rhythms and using rural styles and techniques. He has a natural sense of pace. His songs are a perfect partnership between lyrics and music: they tell real stories and celebrate love and the texture of life in an awe-inspiring balance between intensity and deceptive simplicity. In performance, live and on record, Jara possessed an undeniable aura; he would crack jokes, sing witty songs, dance beautifully and play with mesmerizing focus. His serene and beautiful voice is extremely clear, as if to let you know the words really matter.

The first CD focuses on "canto a lo humano" (Songs of Humanity) a genre of songs about the lives of ordinary people, written according to Spanish verse traditions. It begins with the beautiful **El Arado** (The Plough), about a man whose ox plough furrows the fields as the sun beats down and furrows his brow. Jara's much-loved **El Cigarrito** conjures a vivid cameo of a man on his way to work early in the morning with just the dying embers of a cigarette butt to warm up his day. **¿Qué Sacó Rogar Al Cielo?** (What Did I Get From Praying?) is as close as one can get to traditional canto a lo humano, both in the falling cadences of Jara's voice and in the plucked guitar playing. More of the same is found on the fourth disc. Disc Two includes his magnificent elegy for Che Guevara, **El Aparecido** (The Ghost).

Many of his songs caused political uproar. The playful **La Beata** (The Nun) was banned, while **Preguntas por Puerto Montt** accused the Minister of the Interior of the massacre of poor, unarmed peasants who had built a shanty town on unoccupied land. Jara went on to create a sequence of songs called **La Población**, written with the inhabitants of a Santiago shanty town.

In **Manifiesto**, he prophesied his own death: "song has meaning when it beats in the veins of one who will die singing the real truth". These four discs reveal the genius of this astonishing songwriter who was cut down in his prime, a man who really did give his life and his music for his people.

Jan Fairley

Further listening: Tributo a Víctor Jara (Fonomusic, Spain) brings together musicians from Spain and Latin America, all singing songs by Jara. One of Jara's major inspirations was Violeta Parra whose **Las Últimas Composiciones** (Ans) collected the final songs composed by this remarkable woman, one of Latin America's few female singer-songwriters, before she took her own life.

42

José Alfredo Jiménez

Las 100 Clásicas

BMG Mexico, 2000

José Alfredo Jiménez (vocals), with El Mariachi Vargas de Tecatitlán, La Banda del Recodo, and others.

In June 1950, the first recordings of songs by the Mexican composer, singer, and frustrated professional football player, José Alfredo Jiménez, changed the face of Mexican popular music, probably forever. Today, Jiménez is known all over Mexico by the title of one of his most famous songs, as "El Rey" (The King).

Jiménez arrived in Mexico City in 1936, as a poor, ten-year-old boy from the provinces. The capital was leaving the country behind, the film industry was booming and record companies were looking for artists who could transmit the new nostalgia for *campesino* (country) life. The style of music that responded to this need was called ranchera (country), and Jiménez was undoubtedly its king. He personified the macho man: strong as an ox, generous, spontaneous, passionate, jealous, demanding, selfish and hopelessly lost in the face of a few cruel words from a woman. His message, conveyed with a very Mexican blend of melodrama and kitsch, reveals that suffering can be splendid, that passion and pain are two faces of the same coin and that you can't pretend to sing the ranchera refrain "Ay, ay, ay, ay!" unless you've lived amongst empty tequila bottles, been cruelly rejected by your lover and spent all your money you can't remember where. When Jiménez died in 1973, the phrase written on his tombstone came from one of his most famous songs, **La Vida No Vale Nada** (Life Isn't Worth

Anything) – an order to live every minute to the full.

Jiménez's output was vast, and this two-volume set contains one hundred of his best-known songs, recorded between 1961 and his premature death in 1973. Although he has been dead for nearly thirty years, Jiménez's songs continue to be recorded by both serious musicians and pop idols, and no drunken party anywhere in Latin America is complete without a few verses of **Un Mundo Raro** (A Strange World), a moving ranchera song about impossible love that was famously covered by Chavela Vargas. **Ella** and **Que Te Vaya Bonito** are also favourites, although none of these compete with the sentiments of **El Rey**, the anti-hero's anthem: "With money or without, I always do what I want, and my word is law. I have neither throne nor queen, nor anyone who understands me. But I am still the king".

In this two-volume collection, Jiménez is accompanied by the highly prized El Mariachi Vargas de Tecalitlán, which has also recorded with Linda Ronstadt. When they play ranchera music they offer orchestrated accompaniment to the very simple melodies. Their traditional repertoire of complex, fiery sones de Jalisco recalls the days before mariachi music was watered down by the ranchera repertoire, and the mariachi bands became little more than colourful, tight-trousered accompanists to the ranchera superstars.

In a few tracks on this collection, including **La Que Se Fue** and **Corrido de Mazatlán**, Jiménez is accompanied by the wonderful brass band, La Banda del Recodo, a great Mexican institution. La Banda fill stadium-sized arenas at least three hundred nights a year, and although band-leader Cruz Lizarraga died a few years ago, the tradition continues in the hands of his numerous sons and nephews, and their children and neighbours from the small village of Recodo.

Mary Farquharson

Further listening: Mariachi Reyes del Aserradero's **Sones de Jalisco** (Corason) reveals the sound of the mariachis before they became sidekicks of the matinee idols. On **La Tirana** (Cabaret), Eugenia León covers Jiménez classics and contemporary songs with passion.

43

Tom Jobim

Quiet Now (Nights of Quiet Stars)

Verve/Polygram, 1999

Tom Jobim (guitar, piano, vocals), Elís Regina, Maria Toldedo, Astrud Gilberto, João Gilberto (vocals), Stan Getz, Joe Henderson (sax), Luiz Bonfa (guitar), and others.

When Tom Jobim died unexpectedly in 1994, Brazilians immediately recognized that no one could take his place. Others, such as João and Astrud Gilberto, had made bossa nova famous, but it was Jobim alone who invented the style, slowing down and breaking up what was essentially a samba rhythm. In the process he created the first true World Music craze – where a musical style developed outside the US burst its national boundaries. The results for the music were mixed – it rarely survived the attentions of American studio producers and their taste for massed strings – but it undoubtedly put Brazilian music at the centre of the world stage. In this sense, Jobim has a claim to be the most important musician in Brazilian history.

In the late 1950s, Brazil's rapidly growing and modernizing big cities were natural markets for a new, quintessentially urban sound, and Jobim seemed its personification: urbane, cosmopolitan, strikingly handsome. He christened his new musical style bossa nova, meaning "new wave" and, for a few golden years, until the military coup of 1964 destroyed Brazilian innocence in all kinds of ways, bossa nova was the sound of urban Brazil. Early bossa is as delicate, intimate and beautiful a music as Brazil has ever produced. It was typically played by an individual singer and guitar – João Gilberto, a brilliant Bahian guitarist and crooner being Jobim's original and preferred cover artist – or by a small group usually featuring piano, guitar and soft percussion. The genius of bossa nova's first and greatest US imitator, Stan Getz, was to see that a jazz saxophone was the perfect complement to the Brazilian line-up.

This Verve compilation has so many highlights one hardly knows where to begin. Elis Regina's stunning singing of **Corcovado** (the title track of the Brazilian release), with a catch in her voice that brings tears to one's eyes (she would be dead within a year of recording it)? The jazzier sound, perfectly arrranged, of **Amor em Paz**, **Insensatez** and **O Morro Não Tem Vez**? The lush orchestrations and haunting rhythms of the later, more meditative Jobim, on tracks like **Chansong** and **Meditation**? The only weakness is the over-orchestrated and Americanized version of **Desafinado**.

The album is drawn from all stages of Jobim's lengthy career, and features collaborations with his superbly talented peers: Getz, Gilberto, and singers Maria Toledo and Astrud Gilberto (whose quavering version of The Girl From Ipanema was the first Brazilian international mega-hit in 1961). But two stand out: Elis Regina, whose marvellous voice found a composer worthy of it in Jobim, and the Bahian guitarist Luiz Bonfa, whose jazz duets with Getz are superlative – check out the interplay between them on "Insensatez" and "O Morro Não Tem Vez".

The collection also reveals Jobim's great talents as an arranger and studio producer: he put his training to perfect use in arranging his songs with perfect timing, played by top-quality musicians with not a note out of place. Although he was disarmingly frank about his limitations as a singer, his husky, crooning singing voice perfectly complements the music. A great album, and a fitting memorial.

David Cleary

Further listening: Casa de Mãe Joana (Blue Jackal) is a lyrical compilation of guitar and cavaquinho songs with flute and gentle percussion – the kind of thing the young Jobim would have enjoyed on off-duty nights. **Brazil Roots Samba** (Rounder) covers the old guard of the samba schools from the Rio favelas (shanty towns).

44

Lhasa

La Llorona

Warner Atlantic, 1998

Lhasa De Sela (vocals), Yves Desrosiers (guitar, bass, accordion, banjo, percussion), Mario Legare (double bass), François Lalonde (percussion), Didier Dumoutier (accordion), Mara Tremblay (violin), Jean Sanbourin (sousaphone), Nervous Norman (clarinet).

Journalists and record companies love to put music into nice little categories, but what to do with an artist like Lhasa? Her father is Mexican and her mother American, and she spent her early childhood in upstate New York, before her parents had the idea of showing Lhasa and her siblings "the world". Lhasa was actually home-schooled by her parents on the back of a school bus that made its way from the American northeast all the way down to Mexico. Five years ago, she dropped out of college and moved to Montreal to pursue a singing career. Her music reflects her eclectic, untraditional upbringing: it's rooted in Mexican folk tunes and recorded acoustically with an eastern-European gypsy flair and a touch of Tom Waits.

At times haunting, always moving, the emotionally packed **La Llorona** (The Weeping Woman) is a musical tour de force, and a groundbreaking debut recording. Lhasa and Desrosiers, the album's producer, met in Montreal, Canada and signed to a small Quebec record label, Audiogram. **La Llorona** (The Weeper), their first recording, reflected their tastes and their record collections. It combines Mexican folk music with the intelligence of Tom Waits, the glee of Gypsy music, the soul of Billie Holiday and the passion of Portugal's fado singer, Amália Rodrigues.

Lhasa possesses that rare gift – Cesaria Evora comes to mind – of being able to communicate with those who don't know a word of her language. Her raw emotions transcend all barriers. The album opens with the stunning **De Cara a la Pared** (Face to the Wall), a song filled with passionate pleas to escape from solitude set to a loping beat accentuated by the sounds of a gushing water bottle and an eerie violin. **El Pájaro** (The Bird), a tale of fleeting love, also epitomizes Lhasa's sound. It's perhaps how Tom Waits's music might have sounded if he had sung with a delicate, soulful Latin voice; tempos change and an eerie cloud hangs over this intoxicating yet simple number arranged for guitar, bass, and vocals. **Los Peces** (Fish), an old Mexican folk tale, is given a makeover perfectly matching Lhasa's sumptuous voice with an almost vaudevillian arrangement.

The album is also very representative of the current trend in Latin music in that it explodes beyond the boundaries of traditional genres and styles. Today, groups such as Los De Abajo, with their dynamic blend of rock, salsa and ska, or Colombian rockers Aterciopelados prove that today's top Latin bands can't be simply pigeonholed into boxes labelled "salsa" or "bolero".

La Llorona is remarkably different from most independent first efforts – it was even partly recorded in Lhasa's own kitchen. It never received much radio air-play, but became a cult album by word of mouth – and sales snowballed. In 1997 the album went gold in Canada, and it was released internationally by Warner-Atlantic the following year. The company was confronted with that same problem: what to call a Mexican-American singer who sings in Spanish but who hasn't made a typical Latin record? Wherever the shops decide to stack it, it's a passionate, spine-tingling ride of totally acoustic Mexican folk music. But then, it's not really folk music either…

Dan Rosenberg

Further listening: For another groundbreaking Mexican album that doesn't fit neatly into any musical categories, try Los de Abajo's debut, **Los de Abajo** (Luaka Bop), a mesmerizing blend of ska, salsa and rock. A wonderful example of the growing Mexican underground scene.

La Lupe

La Reina La Lupe

Fania/Sonido/Universal Music, 1998

La Lupe (vocals), with the bands of Tito Puente and Mongo Santamaría.

The Cuban singer La Lupe referred to herself as "La YiYiYi", brandishing such raucous cries to seduce and provoke her fans – the YiYiYis. She would hover over a pianist, chanting like a crazed sorceress, or screech her other catchphrase, "*Ayi Na Ma!*" (Put it there!), as a musician bared his soul in a solo. Picasso called her a genius; Ernest Hemingway declared her "Creator of the Art of Frenzy." Salsa is a conservative nation and Lupe Victoria Yoli Raymond was a wild, wild woman with a strikingly powerful and expressive voice, and a spectacularly uninhibited stage act teetering on madness. "*Yo soy como soy*", she sings, "I am what I am". She was both adored and persecuted for it.

La Lupe came from a poor family in Santiago de Cuba and learned to sing by copying Celia Cruz songs from the radio. She won a radio competition to study music in Havana, and took up a residency at the bohemian Club La Red. She let rip: singing and dancing, kicking off her shoes, improvising risqué verses, tearing at her body and her clothes, she filled the room with frenzy. But she was too much for revolutionary puritans, and she left for Mexico in 1962, before moving on to New York.

A few gigs with Puerto Rican crooner Ismael Rivera added his gloriously chocolatey-erotic **Besito Pa' Ti** to her repertoire. The Cuban conga player Mongo Santamaría produced the album *Mongo Introduces La Lupe*, which took her into the Latin and

American charts. He also introduced her to Tito Puente, and their turbulent relationship (private and musical) yielded the 1965 gold album *TP Swings, The Exciting Lupe Sings* and many hit songs – several are included here. She referred to her greatest hit, the sublime bolero **Qué Te Pedí**, as her "hymn", and Puente gilded it with sparkling vibes. Puente couldn't cope with her increasingly scandalous behaviour, however, and sacked her, so she took off on tour. Venezuela adored her, and she recorded folk songs like **El Adiós**, a llanera from the plains accompanied by softly jangling harps, and, in Andean tradition, the marvellously striking **Golpe Tocuyano**, a brisk, guitar-based joropo, which she sings with a suitably sharp, tangy edge.

This set includes rumba, salsa, flamenco-esque adventures (**María Dolores**), rock'n'roll covers in awkward English and Spanglish (the excruciating **Como Acostombre**) and her favourites, the boleros, where the cracks in her voice are barely controlled. **Se Acabó**, which she translates as "It's over, baby" is clearly of the *Goldfinger* era, and she sounds like a melodramatic, Latino Shirley Bassey. The absence of musicians' credits makes for guesswork, but the racing, brassy mambo, **Menéalo (Tiene El Ajuear Abajo)**, and the fabulous **Yo No Lloro Más** are surely Puente's work.

There is one terrible omission: La Lupe's sensational re-make of Peggy Lee's "Fever", recorded with her then husband, singer Willie García, on which her cackling, witchy Spanglish intro and sexy yelps, scraping vibrato and purring sensuality evoked both Eartha Kitt and Edith Piaf. García banters with her here on the infectious **Qué Bueno Boogaloo**, a brassy, full-tilt Puente production loaded with handclaps and interrupted by a funky percussive rumba. You can just see her gyrate.

Sue Steward

Further listening: La Lupe's **Reina de la Canción Latina** (Tico Records) includes a must-have version of "Fever". Azúcar Letal's **The Next Generation of Afro-Cuban Pop** (Sub-Pop Records) sees three young Cuban women take rap and rock into timba and create what has been described as "mongrel music" and "Electro-timba". La Lupe would have approved.

46

Víctor Manuelle

Sólo Contigo

Sony Tropical, 1994

Víctor Manuelle (vocals), Pedro Pérez (bass), Domingo García (piano), Angie Machado, Cusi Castillo, Luisito Aquino (trumpet), Rafy Torres (trombone), Sammy Velez (baritone sax), and others.

Sólo Contigo (Only With You) represents the apogee of that much maligned and woefully misunderstood style, salsa romantica. Initially derided as flaccid, sentimental pap, the essentially Puerto Rican idiom evolved in the mid 1980s into intense, intimate dance music. It represents a softening of a once macho genre. Established bands, forced to conform, brought to it their standards of musicianship and writing, and found the subtler, mid-paced sensuality of romantica could work to their advantage.

This album is a classic of the genre, a slow burner that reveals its insistent charm slowly on repeated listening. All aspects of its production are first class: beautiful instrumental playing; subtle, indulgent arrangements; seductive lyrics; and a vocal line that never sacrifices its ingenuous sensuality on the altar of melodrama. But as ever it is the quality of the songs – that elusive combination of tune and lyrics – that makes an album memorable. And these are unashamedly and brilliantly commercial.

Victor Manuelle was discovered by Puerto Rico's favourite *salsero*, Gilberto Santa Rosa, who had achieved fame as the singer best able to combine roots appeal with musical excellence; the master unquestionably saw something of himself in the talent and ambition of the young Víctor. In spite of the obvious commercial limitations of the salsa genre, Manuelle now rivals world-famous Latino popsters like Ricky Martin in popularity – in his native Puerto Rico, at least.

This, Manuelle's second album, was a huge hit. Its typical salsa romantica themes are the yearnings and recriminations of lovers, and their inability to reconcile desire with love. The songs are wilfully escapist, but what makes them delicious is the brilliant domination of the romantica genre by everyone involved, not least the canny veteran arranger and producer, Ramón Sánchez.

Manuelle simply pours out his emotions on **Apiádate De Mí** (Take pity on me), **Te Llevo Dentro** (I Carry You Inside Me), and **Sólo Contigo** (Only with you). More sophisticated, perhaps, are the bitter ditties of disillusion: **La Escena** (The Stage) is a tour-de-force of self-righteousness, a superbly realized drama invested with an urgency which belies its pace, always controlled and unhurried.

The outstanding **Voy A Prometerme** (I'm Going to Promise Myself) was written by Manuelle himself. With no small amount of conscious self-deception, he promises himself never to see his girl again, as he lies in their bed, consumed with desire, while she is in the arms of another. **No Alcanzó** (We Didn't Manage) regrets the failure of an affair with more dignity. It is confident enough to set the scene with a reflective mood, building up to the drama-infused mid-paced urgency that characterizes the entire album. Defiance is rarely more attractively packaged than in **Por Ejemplo** (For Example), as Manuelle declares his eyes to be wide open in pursuit of this dangerous, perhaps poisonous lover.

Almost everything in this album is unexpectedly understated. The slick rhythms insinuate, the standard horn configuration of trumpets, sax and trombone adds layers of texture, breaking through only occasionally to hit ecstatic peaks, and the vocals are primarily intimate, avoiding histrionics.

Tommy Garcia

Further listening: Tony Vega's **Si Me Miras A Los Ojos** (RMM) and Raulín's **El Sonero Que El Pueblo Prefiere** (AE), are albums by veterans who adapted to salsa romantica and triumphed.

47

Daniela Mercury

Swing Tropical

Globo-Columbia, 1999

Daniela Mercury (vocals), Toni Augusto (guitar), Cássio Calazans, Cesário Leone (bass), Ramón Cruz (drums), Alfredo Moura, David Santiago (keyboards), and others.

Daniela Mercury burst onto the Brazilian music scene in the early 1990s and quickly became the biggest pop phenomenon in decades. By the end of 1993, her album *Canto da Cidade* was the best-selling Brazilian album by a female singer ever, a record it still holds. That year, she literally brought São Paulo to a halt when thousands of fans trying to get into a lunchtime concert in the city centre provoked a traffic-jam gargantuan even by São Paulo standards.

Mercury's seemingly instant stardom was a breakthrough event in the history of modern Brazilian music, since it marked the new domination of the domestic scene by Bahian pop (from Brazil's northeastern state), which came to be called "axé music". The focus of the new wave was Bahia's capital city, Salvador, with its huge and distinctively Afro-Brazilian Carnival and its local influences of reggae, soca and other Caribbean music. Salvador's more commercial, percussive sound was a natural for the World Music market, and the city has now emerged as a music centre that overshadows even Rio.

Daniela Mercury was the embodiment of all that was best about Bahian music: new beats, an emphasis on live perfor-mance, direct contact with the fans and a strong link with Salvador's Carnival, which is less well known than Rio's but in many ways more street-centred and interesting. Daniela had a refreshingly poppy conviction that music is best enjoyed on your feet, beer in hand, preferably in the middle of a large crowd of like-minded revellers. Star quality oozes from every pore and she is a brilliant live performer with a great voice. What's more, she is a superb dancer – formally trained, with a degree from the first undergraduate dance course in Brazil!

Swing Tropical is a greatest-hits compilation, with tracks from all Mercury's albums, though as they are not arranged chronologically there is little sense of how her style developed. The earliest hit, **Swing da Cor**, gives an instant feel for what makes Daniela special – an insanely catchy up-tempo melody, her fine voice, superb percussion and a stirring mix of Afro-Brazilian and reggae rhythms to drive the beat along. Although "Swing da Cor" was originally cut on an independent Salvador label, it was enough to get Daniela a big recording contract with Sony, whose investment handsomely paid off with the mega-hit **Canto da Cidade**, the opening track on this compilation and easily the biggest Brazilian song of the decade. You can feel its origins as a straightforward Carnival dance smash, but you can also hear what makes it original: the choppy rhythms and Daniela's soaring voice are a perfect match for the heavy percussion. Other tracks in the same vein – such as **O Reggae e o Mar**, **Tá No Batuque** and **Rapunzel**, her smash of the late 1990s – were almost as successful.

A couple of slower tracks from recent records – **Você Não Entende Nada**, for example, and **Rede** – show that there is much more to her voice than Carnival shouting. Songs such as these are perhaps a sign of things to come. Daniela took Bahian pop as far as it could go; it will be worth seeing where she goes from here.

David Cleary

Further listening: Daniela Mercury (Sony) is a reissue of the 1991 debut album, *Canto da Cidade*, which made her a national and international star. Another gifted young singer from Salvador de Bahia, Margareth Menezes, had great success with **Ellegibo** (Polydor), which is occasionally brilliant but also has a few to awful 1980s rock-outs.

48

Totó La Momposina

Pacantó

Nuevos Medios, 2000

Totó La Momposina, Paulina Salgado, Jorge Aguilar, Livia Vides (vocals), Hugo Fernández, Freddy Soto, Adolfo Castro (trumpet), and others.

With a vibrant troupe of singers and dancers, backed by traditional deep bombo drums, stringed instruments, gourd shakers and sweet flutes, Colombian singer Totó la Momposina exposed new international audiences to her country's traditional music. At home in Colombia, her great charisma and ability has transformed attitudes to roots music. While she is no anti-modernist, Totó's concern is for rural rather than urban traditions, and she performs older styles of Colombian music with panache.

The title track, **Pacantó** (For The Song), is a traditional song from a northeast coastal village. It opens with an undulating drum, plucked tiple (a Colombian guitar) and gentle maracas, as Totó's languid tones issue a roll call of local musicians and dancers. The intensity mounts towards the chorus, adding in a growing mix of brass, strings and voices as the dance beat builds. **Goza Plinio Sierra**, complete with a procession of brass and percussion, evokes the *parandas* (street fiestas) in which entire villages, down from the hills, "make the dead feel like dancing."

La Momposina also introduces West African sounds into the mix, her subtle approach creating cross-cultural connections without losing any of the music's original magic. **Milé (El Hombre Borracho)**, which tells the story of a drunkard husband, adds a touch of soukous, courtesy of the Congolese guitarist Papa Noel. The entrancing, mellow final track, **Mami Wata**, also makes West African links, Totó's rich timbres contrasting with the glorious high-harmony voices of Mama Keita and Djank Diabate.

Acompáñala is Totó's inspired dedication to the moon, a country serenade whose infectious rhythms build slowly like a gracious ritual, pared back to foreground the voices of Totó and chorus. It leads into **La Ripiá**, a festival song from the village of San Jacinto in which a continuous ripple of sound is created by the striking, mellifluous tones of the indigenous Colombian gaita flutes. Each flute piece involves the entwined harmonies of "female" (high register) and "male" (low register) instruments (certain songs, such as **El Porro Magangueleño**, were at one time played only by men). **Así Lo Grita Totó** (This Is How Totó Cries) is led by the flute of Nicolás Hernández, who wrote the song in honour of Totó herself.

Many lyrics have a political dimension. **La Cumbia Está Herida** (The Cumbia Is Wounded) celebrates the need to preserve rural cumbia from the challenges of internationalization and political violence – the chorus of "*y nadie protesta*" ("and no-one protests") states her position. **Chambacú**, a brooding track, honours a Cartagena shanty town whose inhabitants struggled for proper housing like their slave ancestors fought for freedom. The song concludes, "you write your own history".

With **Repárala** (Repair Her), Totó passes comment on men wooing women with gifts. But despite such modern attitudes, the song is as traditional musically as most others on *Pacantó* – it's another irresistible dance from the old slave communities. For **Pozo Brillante**, Totó is joined by her mother, and together they sing fabulous improvised verses. It's a fine track of typically confident but unforced musicality, on an album whose every song is memorable.

Jan Fairley

Further listening: Alexis Murillo's **Los Nemus del Pacífico**
(Riverboat/World Music Network) creates gloriously danceable
"montuno colombiano", their swingy rhythm section and rootsy
percussion balancing itself against blasts of brass.

49

Andy Montañez

El Swing de Siempre

TH-Rodven, 1991

No musicians credited.

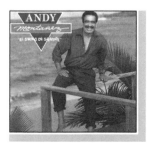

Rarely do you hear a voice that quickens your pulse and elicits a smile of anticipation from the first moment. Andy Montañez, whose emotion-packed, haunting tenor is synonymous with the swing of Puerto Rico, has just such a joyous sound. For almost four decades, he has fronted well-known groups such as El Gran Combo and Dimensión Latina, and has finally emerged as a solo artist of some charisma. **El Swing de Siempre** (Eternal Swing) was a delightfully unlikely and shockingly simple return to form at the beginning of the 1990s, a moment when fashion appeared to have left his molten, outpouring style behind.

While at the peak of fame during the so-called salsa boom of the mid 1970s, Andy Montañez received an astonishing offer from the leading Venezuelan band, Dimensión Latina, who had just lost founder member Oscar D'León to what was to become his brilliant solo career. Rafael Ithier advised the Puerto Rican singer to go for the unprecedented financial certainty, rather than the co-operative of El Gran Combo. This career move – only partially successful – paved the way for the singer's solo career.

To some extent, Montañez had reached and conquered all the heights while with El Gran Combo. The best he could hope for was to be able to find material and arrangements to maintain the standards that had marked him out as one of the truly great singers. The early 1980s saw him do just that, but his searingly dramatic voice, best suited to the driving, attacking style of traditional dance music, didn't fare as well with the more intimate approach of salsa romantica.

The album is a wonderful reaffirmation of Montañez's dedication to salsa dance. The title track, **El Swing de Siempre**, is a reworking of one of his many sensational hits with El Gran Combo de Puerto Rico, updating the original "El Swing" by declaiming slyly, tongue firmly in cheek, that he now offers the same swing – but with more experience. There follows an electrifying, up-tempo romp through territory familiar to all lovers of salsa. The arrangements draw heavily on the signature riffs of Rafael Ithier, pianist and leader of El Gran Combo.

Montañez serves notice of intent with the first track, **Chemen Chemen**, an indulgent celebration of a charming beachbum seducer. The dedication to simple, essential pleasures sets the mood for the entire album. **Voy A Ser Como Papá** – "although Mama won't like it, I'm going to live just like Papa" – and **Pirata de Noche** (Pirate of the night) make this abundantly clear. **Ay Cucu** and **Carolina** are paeans to palpitatingly desirable women, the tunes arranged to allow Montañez to pursue them with his hallmark sensual swing.

El Swing de Siempre truly lives up to its title, with track after track pitched at that uncomplicated, must-dance pace. The session band, with two saxes and two trumpets anchored to a trombone, hark back to the days when El Gran Combo seemed to rule the salsa world. Tight, urgent arrangements back a singer who knows how to build a number, how to provoke the listener with suggestions of his power and depth, and how to release that tension and soar thrillingly away. As Montañez sings, "hang the soft salsa fashions, let's go for swing". And how they all succeed, doubtless with a sense of sweet vengeance.

Tommy Garcia

Further listening: 780 Kilos de Salsa (Edenways), by Dimensión Latina, sees Montañez trading lead vocals with Wladimir Lozano and Rodrigo Mendoza, supported by Cesar Monge's extraordinary lightness of touch in his arrangements for the three-trombone band.

50

Marisa Monte

Verde, Anil, Amarelo, Cor de Rosa e Carvão

EMI, 1994

Marisa Monte (vocals), Gilberto Gil (violão, guitar), Nando Reis (guitar), Carlinhos Brown (percussion), Arthur Maia (bass), Jorginho Gomes (drums), and others.

Brazilian music is often criticized for lacking young stars who can replace the revolutionary generation of the 1960s. While there is some justice to the charge, especially when it comes to the men, an easy two-word rebuttal lies with Marisa Monte. There is a strong argument that the 1990s were the best years ever for Brazilian women singers. Younger singers such as Belô Velloso, Bebel Gilberto and Sílvia Torres had emerged, but head and shoulders above them all was the extraordinary talent and voice of Marisa Monte. And **Verde, Anil, Amarelo, Cor de Rosa e Carvão** – against stiff competition – is her best album.

It is still too early to tell whether Marisa Monte will come to occupy the place of Elis Regina in Brazilian musical history, as the queen of all MPB (Popular Brazilian Music) singers, but it is clear she and Elis are the two finest women singers Brazil has yet produced. They make an interesting contrast: Elis bulldozed her way into the national heart with the raw emotion of her songs and the soap-opera tragedy of her life; Marisa Monte, on the other hand, inspires respect rather than love. Like Elis's, her fabulous talent speaks (or sings) for itself, but where Elis was wildly erratic Marisa Monte is tightly controlled.

Monte has co-produced her own records from the start, maintains her privacy, rarely gives interviews, and spends long periods in New York, where she works with top-drawer producers and studio musicians. Her live concerts are brilliantly professional, the execution of the songs impeccable. But there is no hint of the Piaf-like emotional intensity of the relationship between Elis and her audience. In their own way, each embodies the spirit of their times: Elis the cultural ferment of Brazil in the 1960s and 1970s, Marisa the calmer, more mature 1990s, as democracy took root and Brazilian music and culture calmed down.

Like so many other Brazilian stars, Marisa Monte comes from Salvador de Bahia, but she is also the national MPB star par excellence, rather than a regional singer. Extraordinarily versatile, she sings anything from samba to northeastern genre music, and her range is reflected in the amazing range of collaborators on this disc: fellow Bahian, Gilberto Gil; veteran *sambista*, Paulinho da Viola; avant-garde Salvador composer and percussionist, Carlinhos Brown; roots Rio samba group Velha Guarda da Portela; even New York avant gardist Laurie Anderson. But this is not the foot-tapping dance album that such a list might lead you to believe. It is an incomparably good, laid-back showcase for Brazil's purest, most sensuous voice – a Latin female riposte to Smokey Robinson.

From the opening bars of the first track, **Maria de Verdade**, Monte's voice wraps itself around the melody like a cat, swinging around the beat with perfect pitch and timing, and letting herself go at the end of the song before bringing it to a perfect stop. It is immediately obvious how far ahead she is of anyone of her generation. There isn't a single weak track on the album, but the highlight is probably **Segue O Seco**, a brilliant version of a Carlinhos Brown song with the twang of the Bahian berimbau (fiddle) in the background and that perfect voice slinking around the rhythm and lyric. It is the embodiment of the best of contemporary Brazilian music.

David Cleary

Further listening: Marisa Monte's **Rose and Charcoal** (EMI-Metro Blue) just missed the cut: a meltingly wonderful acoustic set, the material ranges from Paulinho da Viola to Lou Reed.

51

Beny Moré

Cuban Originals - Beny Moré

RCA Original Masters/BMG, 1999

Beny Moré (vocals), Pérez Prado, Nino Rivera (piano), Félix Chappotín, Alfredo "Chocolate" Armenteros (trumpet), and others.

Cuba has never produced a singer as popular or as talented as Beny Moré. When he died, in 1963, Cuba mourned like an extended family. Fidel Castro sent soldiers as pallbearers to his funeral and the Yoruba chants of an all-women choir accompanied him into the next world. Fifty years later, Moré's voice is still the standard by which singers measure themselves – and are measured. His reputation is being maintained by a prolific re-issue industry that is now releasing a stream of CDs like this wonderful sixteen-track compilation of smoochy boleros and brassy mambos and son montunos.

The collection was selected from original RCA recordings made between 1949 and 1958, when Beny was Havana's hottest ticket. He was resident at the fabulous open-air nightclub, the Tropicana, with his own show on Cuban television. This disc possesses the bright tone and clarity associated with recordings from that era, when big bands lived up to their names. One critic described Moré's 22-piece Banda Gigante as "a kind of jazz band with Cuban drums" and this compilation reveals the superb and inventive musicianship in its precise arrangements, all of which had to be dictated by the self-taught singer.

Beny Moré remained a country boy at heart all through his life. His stage accessories of wide-brimmed straw hat and walking stick were mementos of a childhood spent in the sugar-cane growing southeast, and his intricate dance-steps included moves he learned as a child in Afro-Cuban ceremonies. His trademark baggy zoot-suits, however, were a nod to US fashions.

His repertoire recalls his humble beginnings. The upbeat **Santa Isabel De Las Lajas** was his tribute to home, and is delivered as a long, high rap against a hypnotic background of repeated saxophone choruses. **Compay José** continues the nostalgic theme in a tale of eating chicken and rice by the river bank, although it was a lifestyle he had abandoned by 1940, when he moved to Havana. City life finds expression in the frenzy of his four trumpets and five saxophones, a stark contrast with the acoustic trios which launched his voice in the 1930s.

Moré's effortless vocal style was immensely versatile. He could transmit deep, raw emotion in slow, romantic boleros like **Como Fue**, **Tú Me Sabes Comprender** and **Corazón Rebelde**, soaring smoothly and confidently into a high falsetto and covering whole bars like molten gold. "Como Fue" was resurrected by Ibrahim Ferrer with Buena Vista Social Club, but in this original version, Moré gave a unique sense of drama and passion to the lyrics – "your lips or your mouth, your hands or your voice" – with a helpless tremolo, echoed by a muted trumpet.

For the dancing frenzy of mambos and son montunos, Moré adopted a rougher, cruder, more rural edge, as in **Bonito y Sabroso**, **Qué Bueno Baila Usted**, and the classic **Francisco Guayabal**. Dancing was Moré's life, and in "Bonito y Sabroso", he compares the relative merits of Cubans and Mexicans. In **Rumberos De Ayer** (Yesterday's Rumba Players), he pays tribute to Cuba's great Afro-Cuban drummers and laments the death of conga player Chano Pozo, murdered in New York in 1948; Moré sings "Without Chano, I don't want to dance".

Sue Steward

Further listening: The Best of Beny Moré (Sony), taken from a live show on Havana's Radio Progreso, has the bonus of some brief chatty banter between singer and compère. Adalberto Alvárez is the forger of a modern son tradition worthy of Moré; try **Cubania Son 14 with Adalberto Alvárez** (Tumi Music).

Los Muñequitos de Matanzas

Vacunao

Qbadisc, 1995

No musicians credited.

Imagine you're in Matanzas, on Cuba's Atlantic coast. You're at a party thrown by Los Muñequitos de Matanzas, the group that epitomises the hypnotic, raw power of Afro-Cuban rumba. Two wooden clave sticks begin to click out the essential *one-two, one-two-three* rumba beat while a driving rhythm is set up by the cata (a slit wooden tube played with sticks). A fluid male voice launches into an improvised anecdote and is answered immediately by rich choral harmonies. As the rumba opens out, women coquettishly undulate hips and pelvises as they swirl their skirts; men, dressed in white, begin to shake their bodies and shift their feet. Suddenly the verse breaks into a call-and-response routine over pattering rhythms beaten out on three distinctly pitched conga drums – the tumba, llamador and quinto – and the sizzling swishes of the three-headed metal shaker they call the maruga. Such is rumba.

Los Muñequitos – the "Little Dolls" – were formed in 1952 with the idea of providing music for local celebrations. They developed into Cuba's foremost pure rumba group. They are an extended family affair spanning numerous generations, and the depth of their knowledge of rumba is probably unrivalled. Rumba's history stretches back into the days of slavery, when it was the music of resistance for Cuba's black population. And several rumbas still employ African languages that were kept alive by various Afro-Cuban sects (one such is the all-male Abakuá, a

Freemason-like secret society which is celebrated in the slow rumba, **Abakuá Makonica**).

This disc features three forms of traditional rumba, most following the popular cock-and-hen guaguancó form. When the group was first formed, it was known as Guaguancó Matancero, a name which only changed after their first hit, "Muñequitos de Matanzas", became so popular that it had audiences shouting out the phrase at their performances. In the guaguancó dance form, the man tries to "possess" his partner, using gestures of the arm, foot or head to make a symbolic conquest. The woman protects herself by rapidly folding her open hands over her pelvis, then pausing for a moment, before moving on beyond the man's reach – but close enough to drive him on. This game of rumba, a parody of sexual conquest, continues until the man finally makes the final, quick *vacunao* – or "vaccination".

Boxes as well as drums are used for percussion, a throwback to the days when slaves used fish crates from Matanzas port. Three boxes, pitched at tenor, baritone and bass, take the musical roles assumed later by the congas. For the yambú, the oldest, slowest, deepest rumba dance, the Muñequitos use boxes to get the feel; for religious rumba ceremonies they use the sacred batá drums.

El Tahonero is a slow, graceful yambú, in which the three drums interweave around each other. **Wenva** is a gorgeous a capella chant in which different solo leads are answered by the chorus, evoking a powerfully African feel. Rumba's relation to Brazilian samba is expressed on the introduction to **Lengua de Obbara**, while a Spanish influence can be felt in the two-part duo **El Jardín**. But the final song, **Sarabanda**, brings us to the heart of rumba, back to the culture of the Congo from where so many slaves were brought, the chorus singing, "Who plays batá, tambor, bongó? El negro del Congó."

Jan Fairley

Further listening: The raw rumba of today's young Havana can be heard on **Noche de Rumba** (Tumi). The tremendous **Cuba Classics Vol. 3: Rumba** (Tumi) is a historical procession of rumba groups from its roots to sophisticated modern forms.

53

Milton Nascimento

Clube da Esquina 2

EMI, 1994

Milton Nascimento (guitar, vocals), José Carrasco, Danilo Caymmi, Paulo Jobim (flute), Lô Borges (electric guitar), Nelson Angelo, Pato Roves (guitar), Wagner Tiso, Flavio Venturini (keyboards), Jacques Morelenbaum (cello), and others.

The accident of birth which made Milton Nascimento part of the same golden generation as the MPB (Brazilian Popular Music) singers born in the 1940s – singers such as Chico Buarque, Caetano Veloso, Gal Costa and Elis Regina – often leads him to be lumped together with his contemporaries. Yet Nascimento is a distinctive star in his own right. He has arguably the finest male Brazilian voice, a perfectly controlled alto that can soar like no other. And unlike the Bahian and *carioca* (Rio-born) musicians who dominate Brazilian music, he comes from Minas Gerais, the highland area to the north of Rio. It's an area of small cities rather than metropoli, and much more conservative than other parts of Brazil, its popular culture strongly marked by Catholicism. Milton's music reflects his *mineiro* roots in its often slow and complex style, and in the religious elements of his lyrics.

Minas Gerais is a famous breeding-ground for Brazilian politicians, and since Nascimento first burst through to national stardom in the late 1960s his music has been marked by its strong political commitment. He has been a leading spokesperson for the rights of black Brazilians, and he campaigned and sang about the Brazilian Indians a decade before it was fashionable. His musical peak, in the 1970s (this album was first released in 1978), coincided with the worst years of military dictatorship and many of the most famous and durable anti-military songs of the period are his. **Clube da Esquina 2** (The Corner Gang 2) is universally regarded as his masterpiece – a double album released at the height of repression, it is still revered for its quality and integrity.

The openly religious tone of tracks such as **Credo, Paixão e Fé** and **Maria Maria** acted as a smoke-screen to put the censors off their guard, and smuggle in lyrics which are indirect and oblique in their imagery, but pretty obvious in their implications. One such song is **Léo**, one of the less well-known, but most beautiful, tracks on the album. It is a slow, intense number which gives Milton's voice free range to pull at the emotions: "A sidelong glance, a time of war, a straw hut, a name in the hills, a name on a wall, the setting sun, a shot in the dark, a body in the mud...". Several of the songs on this album – **Maria Maria** and **Paixão e Fé** especially – became among the best-known anti-military anthems, and were guaranteed to bring Brazilian crowds to their feet in the late 1970s and early 1980s.

Nascimento was also remarkable for his precocious commitment to the Indian cause – as in the classics **Canoa Canoa**, **Testamento** and **Ruas da Cidade**. But if there is one factor which reveals the unique spirit of *Clube da Esquina 2*, it is the involvement of some of the greatest names in Brazilian music. There are duets with Elis Regina, on **O Que Foi Feito Devera**, and Chico Buarque, on **Canción Por La Unidad de Latinoamérica**, and the list of backing musicians is a roll-call of Brazil's finest. A superb collection from Brazil's most distinctive star.

David Cleary

Further listening: Minas (EMI) is an intense collection marking the break with Nascimento's pop-star days; **Milton e Gil** (Warner) is an excellent collaboration with Gilberto Gil, the other great Afro-Brazilian musician of his generation. Ace vocalist Nana Vasconcelos built a reputation abroad in jazz, rock and salsa collaborations; **Storytelling** (EMI-Hemisphere) is a collection of cool and ambient narratives that express his vision of Brazil.

54

NG La Banda

The Best of NG La Banda

EMI-Hemisphere, 1999

José Luis Cortés (flute, leader, composer), Tony Calà, Jeny Valdés (vocals), Feliciano Arango (bass), Pérez Pérez (sax), and others.

Havana, 2001, and NG – Nueva Generación (New Generation) – La Banda continue to be in the musical vanguard of Cuba's big bands. Few can match the wit and street cred of their lyrics or the inventive arrangements of the band's leader, José Luis Cortés. Before starting NG La Banda in 1988, Cortés had been a key player in the influential Cuban "songo" group, Los Van Van, and he had played flute with the seminal Afro-Cuban jazz group, Irakere.

Much of NG's work goes straight onto DAT recordings made specifically for Cuban radio and isn't heard beyond the island, so this compilation is very welcome. It kicks off with the definitive **Papá Changó**, recorded at a party held in Cortés's own back patio. The emblematic song dates from the early 1990s, when the Cuban population turned in droves to the beliefs and practices of the Afro-Cuban santería cult to help them through the hardships of the "special period" that followed the withdrawal of support from the Soviet Union. Cortés introduces the theme: "Give me light, my father, to overcome harm". The heavy, chunky poly-rhythms are characteristic of the sexually urgent, rumba-influenced timba dance music which emerged at this time.

The contrasting **Verano Habanera** (Havana Summer) is a laid-back serenade to Havana's neighbourhoods at Carnival time, its mellowness echoed by the irresistibly sweet **No Me Molestes Más** (Don't Bother Me Anymore). The infectious **Cara Guante** reveals traces of influence from Panamanian salsa singer Rubén Blades, and is chock-full of cryptic double meanings which draw on the gossip of the Havana scene.

José Luis Cortés structures his music on a jazz model, allowing space for solos from the band members – listen to the extraordinary guitar on **Cienfuegos**. He has an innate ability to turn the opinion of the streets into entertaining yet challenging songs while the infectious choruses get everyone dancing. This is born out in **La Bruja** (the Witch), one of the most controversial Cuban songs of the 1990s, which deals with the emergence of high class prostitution within the island's re-invented tourist economy. Voicing the perspective of a rejected Cuban male, it states the case with head-on passion, performing it in ballad style with saxophone solos and quasi-misogynist choruses, underscored by the wild sound of NG's brass section, the "*metales de terror*". Such machismo is redressed somewhat by the romantic **Veneno**, sung by Jeny Valdés, the first female singer with the new generation of Cuban big bands. Her voice is underpinned by swathes of mambo rhythms inspired by Ravel's *Bolero*.

Ricocheting brass sustain **La Apretadora** (The Squeezer), a teasing dance about the newly assertive Cuban women who are prepared to take men for what they can get and not for who they are. This is followed by a cover of the Beny Moré classic, **Cienfuegos**, with its nostalgic piano introduction. The juxtaposition of this and another Moré cover, **Bonito y Sabroso**, with Cortés's own compelling pieces, reveals him not only to be in the same groundbreaking mould, but also, like Moré, to be an extraordinarily versatile musician. One of the few who can be mentioned in the same breath as the great "Wild Man of Rhythm".

Jan Fairley

Further listening: 1990s compilation **Cuba Now** (EMI-Hemisphere) features Los Van Van, Manolín and Adalberto Alvárez as well as NG La Banda. The son-salsa dance hits of **Juan Carlos y su Dan Den** (Tumi) capture Havana moods, tinged with a salsa-romantica flavour and a trace of edgy timba.

55

Eliades Ochoa

Tributo al Cuarteto Patria

Virgin/Yerba Buena, 2000

Eliades Ochoa (guitar, vocals), Anibal Avila Pacheco (trumpet, claves), Humberto Ochoa, Enrique Ochoa (guitar, vocals), Eglis Ochoa (maracas, güiro, vocals), Roberto Torres (percussion), and others.

There's no mistaking Eliades Ochoa among the old-timers in the Buena Vista Social Club – he's the "youngster" in black, the one in the ten-gallon hat with the Spanish guitar. Away from his home in Santiago, the music capital of Cuba's southeast, Ochoa looks like a man who left his horse behind, but for this celebrated upholder of the Cuban guajira (country music) tradition, it's his guitar that is the faithful companion. He sees it as his link to a long musical tradition and, along with his throaty, rough-edged voice, part of his identity.

In 1999, Ochoa and Cuarteto Patria released *Sublime Ilusión*, featuring Ry Cooder and harmonica player Charlie Musselwhite, who helped the album towards a Grammy nomination. But it is **Tributo al Cuarteto Patria** (Tribute to the "Homeland Quartet") that is Ochoa's most sublime record. It's a delicate collection of the simplest guajiro styles, a showcase for Ochoa's incredible guitar playing and a celebration of Cuarteto Patria's sinuous and rustic songs. On the sleeve, it is described as "a love letter to Cuban music".

Eliades Ochoa received a massive boost from the *Buena Vista* project, but he had been leader of the highly respected Cuarteto Patria since 1978 and had begun busking on the streets of Santiago back in the 1950s. He planned this album to celebrate the group's sixtieth anniversary, and invited past members and others from Santiago's tight musical family to recreate the son, guajiro and guaracha rhythms from their repertoires, adding in some bolero and trova (folk) numbers. It's as Cuban as the tobacco and *guarapo* (cane juice) eulogized in Ochoa's upbeat version of Benny Moré's hit **Yiri Yiri Bon**.

Ochoa amplified the basic *cuarteto* foursome to include his lead guitar, a second harmonizing 'armonico' guitar, double bass and hand percussion (maracas, clave, güiro), and re-introduced the piping tone of the bongos. Delicate, finger-picked guitar solos create rhythmic relationships with the maracas and double bass, and the percussionists weave dense African rhythms into Ochoa's heavily Spanish playing – giving it what Ochoa calls "verve".

Anibal Pacheco drops a couple of carefully placed muted trumpet solos – particularly effective on **Si Sabes Bailar Mi Son** – working with the bongos to create a sinuous, African spirit to Ochoa's improvised Andalucian air. Still in a Spanish vein, Ochoa converts **Que Murmuren** from a tender 1950s Cuban bolero into a poignantly soft flamenco. With **Cuando Ya No Me Quieras**, a melodramatic love song from the 1950s, he introduces an expansive Mexican vocal style.

In spite of all the pensive love songs, Ochoa is, as he sings in **Tiempo Entero**, not averse to a good party. "Another time, another party", as guest of honour, Faustino "El Guayabero" Oramas, sings in his grizzled, 88-year-old voice, delighting in the mischievous lyrics of **Por Culpa De Las Mujeres** (Blame It On The Women). In typical style, Ochoa takes on Guayabero's hit, **Me Voy Pa' Sibanicú**, a fantastic tale about a crazy dog in the mountains, and embellishes it with a long solo from what his sister calls the "pure sweet wires" of his guitar.

Sue Steward

Further listening: On **Cubafrica** (Melodie), Eliades Ochoa and the Cuarteto are joined by one of Africa's most versatile and adventurous musicians, Cameroonian saxophonist Manu Dibango. Vieja Trova Santiaguera have propped up the Casa de la Trova in Santiago for decades with their soft, sweet melodies; go for **La Manigua** (Virgin).

56

Olodum

Popularidade

Warner, 1999

Germano Meneghel, Pierre Onasis, Reni Veneno, Lazinho, Elpidio, Lazaro Negrumy (vocals); no other musicians credited.

Olodum were formed in 1984 in Salvador, capital of Bahia state and of Afro-Brazilian music. They were the cutting edge of axé music, the first and most original of the new groups that, by the end of the 1980s, had transformed Salvador's carnival into the most original in Brazil. Salvador outpaced its rival in Rio for the first time, and Olodum went on to spearhead Bahia's takeover of the Brazilian pop scene. By the end of the 1990s, however, the steam was running out of the Bahian movement as producers increasingly diluted its original, rootsy, African-influenced sound. But by then, the collision between Bahia and Caribbean rhythms like soca and reggae had produced some of the best dance music around.

It was a wave Olodum comfortably surfed from the beginning, becoming the first point of reference for the crowds of international musicians – from Michael Jackson to Paul Simon – who flocked to Salvador in the early 1990s. Olodum's stunningly co-ordinated drumming – with a couple of dozen brightly costumed percussionists whirling drums around their heads and shoulders without missing a beat, set against a backdrop of the cobbled streets and squares of colonial Pelourinho – became an almost obligatory reference point for Brazilian and World Music video-making.

At their best, in the late 1980s, Olodum combined superb

showmanship with real musical originality, mixing African percussion into Brazilian music and popularizing it in a way not seen in Brazil since the development of modern Carnival samba in Rio, in the 1940s. All carnival music is best appreciated live, but **Popularidade** (Popularity) – basically Olodum's greatest hits between 1987 and 1997 – is the next best thing to actually having been to Salvador's carnival during that time. It illustrates all the phases Olodum have passed through, from their superb roots rhythm beginnings, through the commercial success of their high quality pop music, to the decline into over-produced banality aimed at the export market. Fortunately the latter is restricted here to a couple of instructively dreadful tracks – easy to spot, since their English titles are a dead giveaway.

Many of the Olodum drummers came out of the workshop of percussionist and producer Carlinhos Brown, and the earlier tracks feature his heavy use of African rhythms combined with a catchy Brazilian singing style. The two highlights here are **Ladeira do Pelo** and **Farão Divinidade do Egito** – hypnotic, powerful rhythm masterpieces which were smash hits all over Brazil in 1987, the year Salvador's Carnival became a national craze. An even bigger hit the following year was **Nossa Gente (Avisa La)**, a similarly rootsy song, though represented here by a good, poppy Olodum re-recording from 1998.

Other songs from the mid 1990s happily mix together Olodum's percussion base with a series of pleasant Brazilian singers, adding a brass section with a heavy soca influence and some reggae to boot – as in **Requebra**, **Doce Criatura** and **Brisa do Mar**. Three later tracks – notably the compellingly terrible **Smile** – have Olodum on autopilot and gringos in the driving seat. For the rest, get down to the best pop and Carnival music Brazil has produced in the last twenty years.

David Cleary

Further listening: Arakatu, Arakatu (Continental) features more great, carnival-descended pop from Salvador. **Da Mae Africa** (Continental), from the band Reflexu's, is another album of great Salvador roots music in Olodum's wake.

57

Orishas

A Lo Cubano

EMI/Cayo Hueso, 2001

Yotuel "Guerrero" Manzanares, "Ruzzo" (raps), Roldán G. Rivero (guitar, vocals), "Fredo" (scratch mixes), Livan N. Alemán "Flaco-pro" (producer), Anga Díaz (percussion, guitar), and others.

One of Fidel Castro's worst nightmares must have been that Cuba's youth would get into rap, with its adoration of a super-consumerist lifestyle. But as the island opened up to the wider world in the late 1990s, it was inevitable that kids who listened to music coming from Miami and New York would eventually create their own rap scene.

One of the first groups, Amenaza (Threat), featured two rappers known as Ruzzo and Yotuel. Over in Paris, two hip-hop producers, Niko and Flaco-pro, were considering fusing their twin passions for rap and Cuban music, when they saw Amenaza performing in town. The third member of Orishas's vocal front, Roldán Rivero, a traditional Cuban singer, was also appearing at the gig. The five disparate musicians gathered to record a few tracks, and Orishas was born. For **A Lo Cubano** (Cuban-style), they brought in the sensational young conga player Anga Díaz, a graduate of Afro-Cuban jazz band Irakere, as well as Parisian flute, brass and piano players and a silky string section.

Orishas are the Afro-Cuban deities in the santería religion. Each *santero* (practitioner) has an orisha who directs their life; each orisha has its own music, songs and drum rhythms. In the brief intro track, **Intro**, Anga Díaz drums against a solo African chant, and the cultural links between rap and Afro-Cuban music are made. It's a link explored right through this sensationally exciting debut album, which has created a new niche among the US-based salsa and merengue rap fusion groups which emerged in the wake of New York's DLG. And like DLG, Orishas also have a wonderfully soulful voice – in Roldán.

Canto Para Elewa y Chango, which praises the orishas Elewa and Chango, is a sophisticated song which moves between African chants, raps and singing, with a heavy funk bass-line threading brass and piano. It closes in meditative calm, to the sound of shaken seed pods and lightly tapped drums. The santería orishas are a potent force for Cubans, but the appeal of these songs is universal. On stage, in rappers' uniforms (combat pants, t-shirts and dark glasses), they leap and dart and dance around each like their American counterparts, and salsa dance as the DJ injects scratched phrases and the musicians whirl between "straight-ahead" traditional song backings and Bronxese.

Orishas also pay respect to traditional Cuban music. In **Represent** they sing of the former slave barrio of Cayo Hueso, famed for its legions of noted musicians. A deliciously thick bass-line creates a slow, loping swing-beat, like walking through the too-hot streets of downtown Havana, as they sing "my music tastes like the juice of sugar cane".

For Cubans in exile or away from home – like the band themselves (in Paris and Madrid) – certain songs are particularly emotive. **S.O.L.A.R.** (the Cuban tenement blocks once inhabited by slaves and the name of France's premier rapper) name-checks Havana landmarks. **537 C.U.B.A.**, the most straight-ahead song of the set, has obvious resonance as Cuba's international dialling code. Driven by another slow and jaunty bass-line, it is a devastatingly good reinvention of Buena Vista Social Club's world-famous "Chan Chan".

Sue Steward

Further listening: Ozomatli's eclectic Los Angeles sound can be heard on **Ozomatli** (Alma Sounds), an unbeatable, Latin-fusion party album. **Te Gusto O Te Caigo Bien** (Ahi-Nama Records) comes from Bamboleo, the first of Havana's new-wave timba bands to be fronted by female singers.

58

Orquesta Aragón

Cuban Originals – Orquesta Aragón

RCA Original Masters/BMG, 1999

Rafael Lay (flute, leader), Richard Egües (violin), Rafael "Felo" Bacallao, Pepe Olmo (vocals), José Beltran (double bass), Orestes Varona (timbales), Pepe Palma (piano), and others.

El Bodeguero opens this compilation by Orquesta Aragón like a burst of sunshine on a gloomy day. It's hard to imagine a song about a dancing grocer becoming a hit today, but in 1955 it was Cuba's number one and set a standard for every other band in Havana. A version by Nat King Cole, who regularly sang at the famous Tropicana nightclub, began the song's journey around the world and, by the late 1960s, West African stars like Salif Keita, Youssou N'Dour and Papa Wemba were singing Aragón's hits – in phonetic Spanish – in the clubs of Bamako, Dakar and Kinshasa.

Orquesta Aragón was founded in Cienfuegos in 1939 by a local violinist, Orestes Aragón. The group built its reputation on the danzón, a dignified instrumental form whose melodies were carried on flowing violin lines and the melody of a single wooden flute. During the 1930s it seemed the whole population was dancing to the danzón. In 1946, Aragón handed over the band to another violinist, Rafael Lay, who moved it to Havana just as Enrique Jorrín's new invention – the cha-cha-cha – was hypnotizing the city. Jorrín had sharpened danzón's charanga line-up by substituting the more musically versatile and sharp-toned timbales for the tame timpani drums, and adding lyrics. Danzón was just a small syncopated leap away from the cha-cha-cha, and the new form became the vehicle for Aragón's incredible success.

In 1953, Aragón signed to RCA records, the source of these tracks, and a year later, the virtuoso flautist and song-writer Richard Egües joined the band. Egües and Lay were a formidable partnership, and their infectious songs re-shaped Cuban popular music. Titles like **Suavecito** (Little Sweet One) and **Sabrosona** (Delicious Girl) refer as much to the songs' qualities as to the subject's. Taken at a steady pace, "Suavecito" is mostly a showcase for Egües dashing flute; "Sabrosona" is an astonishing song. Opening with Egües's high, trilling flute, which can resemble a human whistle, the violins jump around the melody as a block, creating a jaunty swinging rhythm. The all-male chorus also sings as one, both with and against the violins – unison choruses were part of Jorrin's revolution and became Aragón's trademark. The danzón's stop-start rhythm is retained in a sharply rattled cowbell. The excitement explodes as the tune is repeated by the flute, violins, then whistled by the chorus. And before it turns saccharine, the *timbalero* lashes out with a loud, jerky, clattering drum solo.

The upbeat cha-cha-chas are interspersed with other Cuban rhythms and formats. Love songs, essential in every Latin repertoire, include the classic **La Gloria Eres Tú**, crooned solo to a mellow flute, and the self-pitying **Culpable Soy**, whose singer is consoled by briskly swishing cymbals and the pianist's trilling, flute-like style. In contrast, the country guajira of **Al Vaivén De Mi Carreta** creates the type of song beloved of nostalgic city-dwellers, dropping buzz words like *bohío* (thatched hut) and *carreta* (ox cart). The singers whistle and sing calls to farm animals and pizzicato strings move at a rolling cart's pace. Like the imaginary sugar-cane fields of **Ritmo de Azúcar** (Sugar Rhythm), Orquesta Aragón are as Cuban as rum.

Sue Steward

Further listening: Orquesta Aragón and Fajardo y su Orquesta
(Latin Roots/WS Latino/Sony) **is a double bill of flute-led delights from the pioneers plus Fajardo's later versions. El Manicero: 25 versions of The Peanut Vendor** (Tumbao Cuban Classics/Blue Moon, Spain) unimagineable varieties of this world favourite.

59

Johnny Pacheco and
Pete "El Conde" Rodríguez

Tres de Café y Dos de Azúcar

Fania, 1973

Johnny Pacheco (flute, leader), Pete "El Conde" Rodríguez (vocals), Larry Harlow (piano), and others.

Johnny Pacheco has been paired with the greatest names in New York salsa since the mid-1960s launch of his Fania label. The prodigiously talented producer and multi-instrumentalist started out playing tambora, the drum which powers the traditional merengues of his home country, the Dominican Republic, but Pacheco took up Cuban percussion after moving to New York aged eleven. His first recordings were with jazz musicians like Stan Kenton, but in the late 1950s he joined a quartet with fellow Cubanophile, pianist Charlie Palmieri.

In 1954, a New York concert by visiting Cuban flute player José Fajardo brought Pacheco and Palmieri face to face with the authentic charanga line-up, and they transformed their own group in imitation. Pacheco now switched to the wooden Cuban flute and Palmieri renamed the group La Duboney. The response was sensational, but Pacheco left after six months to form his own band with a more upbeat, rhythmically charged sound. In 1964, with lawyer and Cuban music aficionado Jerry Masucci, Pacheco launched Fania Records, the label which would shape and define Latin dance music for the next 25 years.

Johnny switched instrumental tracks again, from the sweetness of charanga to the brash conjunto style perfected by Cuban tres guitarist Arsenio Rodríguez. He positioned two trumpets out front and installed a tres guitar to work both solo and harnessed to the piano. A sharp percussion section drove the band. This format became the key to Fania's – and Pacheco's – new identity.

In 1963, Pacheco met the Puerto Rican-born New Yorker, Pete Rodríguez, who was known as "El Conde" (the Count) because of his classy, handsome looks. El Conde's smoky, musky voice perfectly matched his image and lent his songs an air of musical dignity – as well as great sex appeal. The two debonair men shared a penchant for silky shirts, Cuban music and cigars, and their partnership lasted – on and off – until El Conde's death in 2001. The title of their 1970 record, *La Perfecta Combinación*, sums up their musical partnership, but it is their 1973 album, **Tres de Café y Dos de Azúcar** (Three of Coffee and Two of Sugar – a reference to the distinctive Cuban rhythm), that is the best momento of their time together

The ten songs have a Cuban bias, from rolling, melodious son and percussive Afro-Cuban rumba to the classic bolero, **La Gloria Eres Tú**. Off the Cuban menu, **Los Diabolitos** is a racing merengue driven by the thrum of the tambora and a coursing piano. On the brisk **Cositas Buenas**, the tres adopts a sterner tone in dialogue with Larry Harlow's piano. Harlow was a prized arranger at Fania and provides an appropriately rhythmic solo on the opening song, **Primoroso Cantar**, about the Afro-Cuban guaguancó rumba. The piano-and-tres relationship explored all through the disc is particularly effective on the jaunty **Son Labori**, where the tres takes off on a spectacular extended solo. But the focal point is always El Conde's extensive vocal range, which Pacheco tries and tests all through the album. He never sounds more aristocratic than on the bolero **Bajo El Viejo Cristal**, which measures time in long, lazy trumpet notes and the singer's languid style.

Sue Steward

Further listening: Pacheco y Su Charanga (Fania) features the early hits; **Celia and Johnny** (Fania) is a golden collaboration, with Celia Cruz on tremendous vocal form on a set of songs straight from the Cuban book.

60

Andy Palacio

Keimoun

Stonetree Records, 1995

Andy Palacio (vocals), Alexander Aranda (Garifuna drums, vocals), Bernard Higgins Higinio (turtle shells, vocals), Dale Aranda (maracas, vocals), Yadam Glez (bass, keyboards), Josvanni Terry (sax), Dafnis Prieto (drums), Norberto Rodríguez (guitar).

If you travel in the Americas – Cuba, Haiti, Brazil and scores of other places – you'll find the sights, sounds and tastes of Africa, a legacy of centuries of the slave trade. And all along the Caribbean coast of Belize, Guatemala and Honduras, small Garifuna settlements maintain distinctly African cultures. How the Garifuna ended up there is a curious story: five hundred years ago, a slave ship was wrecked near the Caribbean island of St Vincent, discharging its cargo of (mostly African) slaves, who stayed on the island for generations, mixing with the native Arawak Indians. Today the modern Garifuna language is a mixture of African tongues and Arawak – and one of the only languages spoken by black populations in the Americas that is not derived from Europe.

In March 1797, after the British conquered St Vincent to make room for tobacco and sugar cane plantations, the new colonizers, frustrated with their uncooperative Garifuna subjects, exiled the entire population. The Garifuna, who numbered around four thousand, went first to Jamaica and later to Honduras; half died during the passage. Since then, they have spread along the Caribbean coast of Central America, and are a major cultural element in Belize. In the evenings, local bars in cities like Dangriga and Belize City are filled with punta rock, a mix of pop music and Garifuna culture's traditional paranda drum rhythms. Indeed, punta has swept Belize to such an extent that it has become a sort of national music. Imagine a blend of soca and salsa set to an almost West-African drumming style.

The region's leading punta rocker is Andy Palacio, who built his reputation by blending Garifuna drum sounds and pop to produce some of Belize's biggest hits. In 1995, he recorded **Keimoun** (Beat On), probably the most ambitious punta album to date. For the recording, Palacio and Stonetree Records' producer, Ivan Duran, went to Cuba's Generator Studio with Cuban musical director Yadam González. The concept driving the sessions was to record punta rock from a Cuban perspective, adding a brass section and leaving space for Latin jazz-inspired solos, with touches of Norberto Rodríguez's guitar work to spice up the mix. *Keimoun's* line-up reflects standard punta – with its Garifuna barrel drums, turtle shell percussion, bass and guitar – but limits its reliance on electric keyboards and adds more brass.

One of the outstanding tracks is **Nabi**, a punta version of a classic composition by Paul Nabor – a leading *parandero* (paranda musician). Nabor adds a Havana-style brass section led by Cuba's Yosvanni Terry to his trademark paranda sound, resulting in a haunting mix of West African guitars and percussion with a Latin jazz flair. Other Havana-born elements are the Cuban guitar and brass solos, neither of which are typical of most puntas. The idea is brilliantly executed on tracks such as **Se Busca**, a song about a smuggler who has arrived with a cargo of goodies from Barranco – Palacio's birthplace – and **Lamiselu**. *Keimoun* also features four Garifuna a capella vocal tracks, songs that recall the music's roots in West African call-and-response vocals and assert Garifuna's presence at the heart of modern punta.

Dan Rosenberg

Further listening: On **Costa y Calor** (Costa Norte), Honduran composer Guillermo Anderson sings punta primarily in Spanish, mixing Garifuna-style percussive layers with the distinctively Central American trova (folk) style.

The Rough Guide to Central American Music (World Music Network) features a broad range of styles, including punta, paranda and trova.

61

Charlie Palmieri

A Giant Step

Tropical Buddha, 1984

Charlie Palmieri (piano), Bobby Rodríguez (bass), Mike Collazo (timbales), Johnny "Dandy" Rodríguez (bongo), Frank Malabe (congas).

Charlie Palmieri, one of Latin music's greatest pianists, was as comfortable playing formal Latin jazz as kick-heels salsa, and equally at home jamming leading a New York *barrio* (neighbourhood) work-shop. His effervescent character and piano playing, and his inexhaustible love of rhythm, transformed everything he touched. His style is instantly recognizable, and utterly different from his brother Eddie's intellectual approach.

The Palmieri family grew up in the Bronx, blessed with a mother who believed in their talent and found money for piano lessons. They graduated from talent contests to playing dances in Puerto Rican social clubs while still at school. Charlie (born in 1927, nine years before Eddie) also studied at the Juilliard Institute. By the age of twenty, he was established on New York's dance-hall circuit, playing Cuban rumbas, Argentinian tangos, and Mexican and Spanish music.

Charlie's passion was Cuban music, particularly the danzones recorded by Arcaño y Sus Maravillas, whose band featured the sensuous double bass of Israel "Cachao" López. In 1954 Cachao performed in New York with flautist José Fajardo's charanga band, and Palmieri – who was then running a Latin-jazz quartet with Johnny Pacheco – was smitten. In 1959, he founded Charanga Duboney, with Pacheco on flute, and launched a craze which lasted into the next decade. Between 1961 and 1966,

Palmieri organized the Alegre All-Stars, a series of descargas (jam sessions) between like-minded soloists. But of all the instrumental configurations Palmieri explored, the quartet was musically most rewarding. With a double bass player and three percussionists from some of New York's most sophisticated dance and Latin jazz bands, the pianist was at his most relaxed. **A Giant Step** was his milestone release, and marked a triumphant return to music after a stroke two years before had paralyzed his left side.

Palmieri pumps up the adrenalin to dangerous levels in the descarga, **Start the World, I Want to Get On**. Bobby Rodríguez's clearly outlined bass notes and Mike Collazo's light-fingered timbales stick-work establish a reassuring backing while the pianist builds excitement with a repetitive four-note riff, then suddenly explodes into a high, white knuckle crescendo.

Fiesta A La King, a Puente mambo, opens with a swirling flourish echoing Palmieri's infectious laughter, and builds to fiesta pitch. The wonderfully melodious **Mis Amigos E.G.C.** begins with a tumbling outburst of scales, in a tribute to Puerto Rico's most famous group, El Gran Combo. Puerto Rico is also conjured in the danza (the equivalent of Cuba's danzón), **Bajo Las Sombras De Un Pino**, whose old-fashioned military beat is laid out in crisp snare-drum rolls punctuated by formal pauses that commemorate the danza's European origins. Its snappy swing is at times pure cha-cha-cha. Brother Eddie is honoured in **Muñeca**, a typically complex piece of Latin jazz.

The closing nine expansive minutes of **Rhumba Rhapsody** are threaded with references to Rachmaninov in its descending keyboard flights and in Palmieri's unusually assertive technique. As always, he inhabits the whole keyboard, greedy for its textures and tones. This album is a superb memorial to a life-enhancing personality, who died, too soon, in 1988.

Sue Steward

Further listening: Viva Palmieri (Sonido) comes from the early days of Charlie Palmieri and Charanga La Duboney; **Alegre All Stars Vols 1–4** (Sonido) brings together New York's most influential soloists in a series of late-night jam sessions led by Charlie Palmieri.

62

Eddie Palmieri

The Best of Eddie Palmieri

Fania Salsa Classics/Charly Records, 2001

Eddie Palmieri (piano, leader), Charlie Palmieri (electric organ), Cheo Feliciano, Ismael Quintana, Tony Vega (vocals), Israel "Cachao" López (bass), Alfredo "Chocolate" Armenteros (trumpet), Manny Oquendo (percussion), Cal Tjader (vibes), Barry Rogers (trombone), and others.

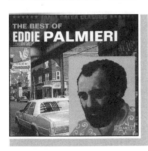

Pianist, bandleader and multiple Grammy-winner, Eddie Palmieri is a survivor of Latin New York's salsa heyday. As one of Latin music's most inventive composers and most experimental pianists, Eddie was never over-shadowed by his elder brother Charlie, who was already a star on the Latin circuit when Eddie was still having piano lessons. His early ambitions as a percussionist led to his characteristically punchy piano style and gave him an uncanny instinct when it came to choosing the rhythm section – two significant acolytes are the *timbalero* Manny Oquendo and Puerto Rican conga player, Giovanni "Mañenguito" Hidalgo. Both appear on several numbers on this excellent two-CD compilation of Palmieri classics.

When Eddie was 21, he joined the singer Tito Rodríguez – Puente's rival for the title of Mambo King. But, restless for musical control, he left in 1959 to form his own band, giving it the immodest but not exaggerated title of La Perfecta. An eight-piece, it included Manny Oquendo, who introduced him to Cuban music, and trombonist Barry Rogers, who introduced him to jazz. Charlie dubbed it a "trombanga" (trombone-charanga). **Muñeca**, **Azúcar**, **Si Echo Pa'lante**, and the stunning **Bamboléate** all represent that trombone-fixated debut. The last track features West Coast "Cool jazz" vibes player, Cal Tajder, in an uncharacteristically brisk encounter with Eddie's piano, in delicate mood, backed by two trombones and sizzling percussion.

At the end of the 1960s, Palmieri discovered the final element in the creation of his original piano style when he was introduced to the Schillinger system of composition, a complex mathematical system which forms the basis of his long, wildly inventive solos (heard on **Lisa** and the opening reverie on **Muñeca**). Palmieri's solos typically unfold in sparkling clusters of staccato chords and long lyrical passages – listen to **Azúcar**.

The three decades covered here (1964–1987) chart his changing musical style. The slow-burning opener, **Ay Qué Rico**, dispels any fears that boogaloo dumbed down Latin music, featuring Israel "Cachao" López's chunky, soft bass-lines, Barry Rogers' sensually stretched trombone lines, plus choruses of "Sock it to me!" and sweet, soulful vocals from Cheo Feliciano. The all-time favourite, **Café**, a shamelessly sentimental reverie about Grandma's coffee, is a long, lazy groove created by piano and trombones.

La Perfecta folded in 1968. Eddie set up a new band and brought in a new vocalist, Lalo Rodríguez, who brought a tougher tone to the band's faster, more urban sound of the 1980s. Two trombones are now augmented by saxes and two trumpets. In 1983, Palmieri moved to Puerto Rico and picked up three Grammy's for albums recorded there. *La Verdad/The Truth* alone yielded several hits and saw Eddie reveling in lengthy, radical solos. He hired local star vocalist, Tony Vega, who enhances **El Cuarto** and **La Verdad** with his unmistakable nasal country twang. At the start of the new century, Palmieri is still going strong; a pioneer still pioneering – and still winning Grammys.

Sue Steward

Further listening: En Aquellos Tiempos (Disco Hit), by 1980s Puerto Rican super-group Batacumbele, features one-time Palmieri conga-man, Mañenguito, on a set of Latin-jazz influenced by Puerto Rican plena and bomba. **Oro Salsero 20 Éxitos** (Rodven) is an excellent greatest hits album from another ex-Palmieri band member, crooner Lalo Rodríguez.

63

Paracumbé

Tambó

Ashe Records, 1997

Emanuel Dufrasne González (barril drums, accordion, trombone, leader), Nelie Lebrón Robles (vocals, percussion), Héctor Calderón (barril, percussion, vocals), Ramón Gómez (pandereta, vocals), Angel Luis Reyes (marimbola), Yamir Ríos (pandereta), Sara Rosado, Rhenna Lee Santiago (vocals), Ivonne Torres (ouatro).

As so often in the Americas, Puerto Rico's music was fundamentally shaped by the slave trade, and among the island's Afro-Puerto Rican styles, bomba and plena are the most prominent genres. Paracumbé is one of the leading "folklórico" revival groups, and while the word may suggest artificial, tourist-oriented music to English ears, the reality on the ground is very different. **Tambó** is simply the best album of bomba and plena recorded. The bomba, with roots in West Africa, is thought to have originated when slaves from different plantations were allowed to gather and celebrate together. Its instrumentation is comprised entirely of percussion instruments: two barrel drums (called barril primo and barril segundo), a pair of hardwood sticks called cuas, and maracas.

Paracumbé's bombas, sung entirely by women, are beautiful call-and-response songs that originated in the southern part of the island. Puerto Rico is divided by a mountain range that made it easier, in the past, to get from Haiti to Puerto Rico by boat than it was to cross from north to south. As a result, the bomba of the south was heavily shaped by the music of Haiti, as distinct from the bomba style of the north which is sung by men.

The album begins thunderously with the bomba, **Cico Mangual**, its orchestra of drums setting the tone for a magnificent series of call-and-response vocals between the fiery Nelie Lebrón Robles and a trance-inspiring female chorus. The song pays homage to Cico Mangual, a legendary bomba dancer from Ponce in the south of Puerto Rico, the town that was the birthplace of the plena. Many other songs on this album are plenas, a style that began its life as a sung newspaper. *Pleneros*, like medieval troubadours in Spain, would travel the island, bringing the news of the day to the public through their songs.

Paracumbé's leader, Emanuel Dufrasne believes that the plena's origins are a result of the fusion of bomba rhythms with forms brought to Puerto Rico by immigrants from Jamaica, Barbados and Trinidad. The new style incorporated many European elements, including a wide range of new instruments such as the güiro (a wooden scraper), the pandereta (a tambourine without jingles), the cuatro (a small guitar) and, later, accordions. A perfect example is **Sueño, Sueño**, where Dufrasne's subdued accordion lays the framework for Robles's passionate vocal description of the dreams of a *cagueño* – a peasant farmer.

In a departure from the stunning female vocalists who dominate the rest of the album, Robles passes the microphone to her male comrades, Ramón Gómez and Héctor Calderó, on **Guañeco Pie**. It's a flirtatious plena, filled with dynamic cuatro and percussion solos, about a sexy dancer named Guañe.

While the plena style more commonly heard today is blasted out by salsa-plena fusion bands such as Plena Libre and New York's Libre, Paracumbé's rootsy versions are a direct link to the genre's origins in West Africa. Simply put, Paracumbé's *Tambó* is Africa in Puerto Rico.

Dan Rosenberg

Further listening: Plena Libre launched the plena revival with **Juntos y Revueltos** (RykoLatino), which features their typical blend of traditional percussion with a salsa edge. Rodolfo Nava Barrera is one of the most important Puerto Rican composers; **Nava** (RykoLatino) showcases his deep smoky vocals in a dynamic fusion of Latin styles with jazz and rock.

64

Chichi Peralta y Son Familia

Pa' Otro La'o

Caiman, 1997

Chichi Peralta (vocals, leader), Jandy Féliz (guitar, vocals), Francisco Ulloa (accordion), "Jhonny" Chocolate (tambora, timbales), Felipe Sánchez, Orlando Cordero, Manuel Tejada (piano, keyboards), London Symphony Orchestra (strings), and others.

Occasionally, an album comes along that touches the heart and soul of a generation. In 1997, Chichi Peralta's **Pa' Otro La'o** (On The Other Side) emerged and ever since it has become impossible to go anywhere in Latin America without hearing it. From the nightclubs of Santo Domingo to the cafés of Caracas, and on radio stations across the Caribbean – odds are, you'll hear the sounds of Chichi Peralta.

The young percussionist from Santo Domingo, the capital of the Dominican Republic, built a tambora drum (the lead rhythm instrument in traditional merengue) when he was four. His father began to teach him about music, and exposed him to a wide range of styles, including classical music, Dominican merengue and bachata, and Cuban boleros and mambos. Peralta's first professional foray was with the small Dominican band, Los Fragmentos, which led him into studio session work as a percussionist and arranger. It was then that he met the giant of Dominican music, Juan Luis Guerra, and began an eight-year stint in 4:40, Guerra's hit group.

After 4:40, Peralta set out to create a new sound which he describes as *fuson* – a dynamic melange that takes merengue, bachata and son, and adds touches of gospel, jazz, blues, R&B and salsa, plus electronic dance music, symphonic textures and percussive layers from Africa, Brazil and Asia. But at heart, Peralta describes himself as a *sonero* – a singer of the local son (a close cousin of Cuba's song style). He founded the group Son Familia and recorded *Pa' Otro La'o* in 1997, bringing together the London Symphony Orchestra and the reggae-gospel group Inner Circle. He added the voice of the glorious Miami soul diva, Betty Wright (on **Un Día Más**), and a collection of the Dominican Republic's greatest musicians and songwriters, including the critically acclaimed guitarist, vocalist and composer Jandy Féliz, who wrote half of the music on the album. It became a landmark recording.

In the opening number, **Amor Narcótico**, Féliz sings about love in a long, musically inventive number that opens on a delicate guitar-and-voice bachata, then is joined by strings and transformed by the appearance of the percussionists into an upbeat celebration – very much in the 4:40 mould. **Ella Tiene** launches with cinematic romantic strings and, typically, adopts several musical guises to tell its story. **La Ciguapa** brings in Inner Circle and builds to a wonderfully infectious cocktail of ragga, merengue and rap with distinctive flavours of soca and salsa – a true Latin-Caribbean dance number. In contrast, Féliz's touching **Limón Con Sal** sees Peralta incorporate elements of American gospel and R&B with bachata. Its title, "Lemon With Salt", refers to the pain and suffering that come at the end of a relationship.

Another Féliz composition, **Procura**, is a love song, a song of temptation and a magical mix of merengue and 1930s Cuban son in the tradition of the Trío Matamoros – with a dash of R&B. *Pa' Otro La'o* is filled with brilliant arrangements and unforgettable songs that are now anthems throughout Latin America. Not surprisingly, it elevated Chichi Peralta to the status of superstar.

Dan Rosenberg

Further listening: Putumayo Presents República Dominicana (Putumayo) is a great introduction to bachata and merengue; including tracks by Luis Vargas and Chichi Peralta. **Píntame** (Sony) features merengue idol Elvis Crespo, whose voice moves easily from speed to smooth.

65

Astor Piazzolla

Luna

EMI-Hemisphere, 1992

Astor Piazzolla (bandoneón), Daniel Binelli (bandoneón), Horacio Malvicino (guitar), Gerardo Gandini (piano), José Bragato (cello), Hector Console (double bass).

Tango musicians have always been in danger of being overshadowed by the provocative dancers or haunting singers they accompany, but tango's *bandoneonistas*, players of the awkward 71-button accordion known as the "Voice of Tango", provide a vital aspect of the sound. Most astonishing and controversial of these was Astor Piazzolla, whose revolutionary compositions incorporated ideas from modernists like Bartok and Stravinsky. He was blackballed by the tango community for decades but found fanatical audiences in Europe and the US. By the time of his death, in 1992, his compositions were performed in jazz and classical programmes all over the world.

Piazzolla was born to Italian-Argentinian parents in Buenos Aires but spent his childhood in New York. In the 1940s, he returned to Buenos Aires and played in the huge tango orchestra of *bandoneonista* Anibal Troilo. A natural restlessness led him to Paris to study classical music under Nadia Boulanger, who encouraged him to merge his passion for jazz and classical music with tango. His compositions always reveal the unmistakable swaying melancholy and unpredictability of tango, however much he protested that "for me, tango was always for the ear rather than the feet".

These seven pieces were performed at Piazzolla's last concert recording, in Amsterdam, in 1989. The hand-picked "New

Tango Sex-Tet" was an unconventional line-up for Piazzolla, who had made his name with quartets, but the darker mood of the cello, which stands in for violin, and the overall sombre tones seem appropriate to this late stage of his life. He added another bandoneón to relieve the strain, but his unstoppable, careening solos and formidable energy are undiminished as the solos rise and fade off without interrupting the tight ensemble flow.

Hora Cero – that ungodly time between midnight and dawn – is a dramatic, monochrome soundtrack to a walk through the backstreets of Buenos Aires. The group evokes catcalls, sighs of pleasure, gasps of fear and flashes of sensual tango melodies emerging from late-night bars. A sense of urban tension is maintained by Piazzolla's staccato choruses and pianist Gerardo Gandini's spare treble cascades. The ten-minute **Sex-Tet** is another complex ensemble piece, with Piazzolla's chameleon-like bandoneón unleashed. In contrast, **Milonga del Ángel** shows Piazzolla in mellow mood; the almost unbearably sustained notes, and the fluttering short phrases that barely stretch the bellows, are shadowed and softened by the cello and piano – then Piazzolla plunges off in dramatic swoops and dives.

The eleven-minute-long **Camorra 3** shows Piazzolla at his most virtuoso: as a cello and piano duet in fast, choppy exchanges, he launches dramatically into an outburst of rage and desire, then just as suddenly stops. The classically organized **Preludio y Fuga** reflects Piazzolla's faith, as he endows his bandoneón with the tone and grandeur of a church organ in a profound solo, while ghostly tango airs recall memories of the flesh. **Luna** (Moon) is an epic masterpiece, a journey through the contrasting landscapes of the composer's imagination. "Tango", Piazzolla said, "is emotion in motion, in rhythm; it is passion".

Sue Steward

Further listening: The Rough Guide to Tango (World Music Network) covers tango's history, from golden era singers such as Carlos Gardel, through to Piazzolla and modern singers such as Adriana Varela. **Rough Dancer and Cyclical Night** (American Clave) is Piazzolla's brilliant departure into New York's avant garde – only for tango adventurers.

66

Omara Portuondo

Buena Vista Social Club Presents Omara Portuondo

World Circuit, 2000

Omara Portuondo, Ibrahim Ferrer, Pío Leyva (vocals), Rubén González (piano), Orlando "Cachaíto" López (bass), Manuel Galbán, Eliades Ochoa, Compay Segundo, Benito Suárez (guitar), Gilberto "Papi"' Oviedo (tres guitar), and others.

Elena Burke, Moraina Secada and sisters Haydee and Omara Portuondo were Cuba's first girl group, pin-ups all through the exhilarating decade that led to the revolution, and for some years beyond. Their four-part vocal harmonies, choreographed dance routines and spangly cocktail dresses dazzled audiences at famous Havana nightspots such as the Tropicana.

Omara left for a solo career (Las D'Aida folded) and over the next few decades, her controlled, smokey voice unleashed its powers on boleros, jazz standards, and songs in the upbeat, jazz-influenced style known in Cuba as filín (feeling) because of its sentimental manner. On stage in Havana's cabaret bars, Portuondo possesses that unpredictable feline edge shared by Eartha Kitt and Edith Piaf. In 1996, she was invited to sing on a session with the young *salsero* Issac Delgado at the EGREM studios, and there met an old friend, Compay Segundo, who asked her to join him on a couple of songs in another studio. From the moment she walked in, her future was transformed. She had unwittingly joined the Buena Vista Social Club.

By the end of 2000, Omara had toured Europe, appeared at New York's Carnegie Hall, received a Grammy, made a heart-warming appearance in Wim Wender's film, and was on the road with her own show. For her solo album, the Buena Vista team (minus Cooder) reconvened in the same studios, and Omara produced eleven songs around her favourite theme – love's tragedies. The combination of her voice and the music accompanying it leaves you inspired and uplifted.

While Omara's solo voice is the focus of the record, there are endless exciting instrumental moments: Manuel Galbán's electric guitar solos in **Canta lo Sentimental**, for instance, "Guajiro" Mirabal's plaintive trumpet in the opening lament, **La Sitiera**, and Cachaíto's pliable bass-lines, which thread the whole disc. The latter come into the open in the introductory duet on the affecting **Veinte Años**, alongside Jesús "Aguaje" Ramos's slinky, muted trombone.

Omara's duets are now world-famous, her contralto texture and perfect timing enveloping the rhythms effortlessly. She harmonizes beautifully with her two leading men – Pío Leyva's high tenor and Ibrahim Ferrer's sexy, bluesy tones. In **Ella y Yo**, with Pío Leyva, she is backed by the rumble of bongos, and two clarinets lend a classical air. With Ibrahim Ferrer, she recreates an old Arsenio Rodríguez classic, **No Me Llores Más**. Their voices, as entwined as the memories of the couple in the song, are serenaded by Rubén González's rolling accompaniment. He must be delighted to reprise his role in Rodríguez's original version, and breaks away for a tantalizingly brief solo, subtly shifting the rhythm around, reminding us of his brilliance.

The Portuondo repertoire isn't all smoochy boleros and pensive rhythms, and includes some frisky dance numbers – guarachas, son montunos, a bolero-cha and a stomping mambo version of Beny Moré's classic **¿Dónde Estabas Tú?** – to take her back to the nights when Las d'Aida shared the Tropicana stage.

Sue Steward

Further listening: Omara's close-harmony group left behind one album, **Cuarteto Las D'Aida** (EGREM), recorded in Havana in the 1950s. One of Omara's favourite songwriters, a legend in Cuban music, is honoured on **Tributo a María Teresa Vera** (Nubenegra/Intuition), a collection of covers of Vera's intense and painfully romantic love songs.

67

Tito Puente

50 Years Of Swing

RMM Records, 1997

Tito Puente (timbales, vibes, leader, composer), and the roll call of salsa musicians.

The death of Tito Puente in May 2000 marked the end of a long chapter in Latin music. The charismatic, bi-cultural, "beans 'n' burgers" Puerto Rican-American, "El Rey" took Latin music into a wider market and his death was mourned by millions of fans worldwide. He also left a void in jazz, a connection apparent throughout this comprehensive three-CD box set, which captures his six-decade career.

Guest jazz soloists including George Shearing, Woody Herman and James Moody reveal how Puente's Latin percussion and inventive brass arrangements reinvigorated big band jazz. The greatest musical moments, though, are those with the most illustrious names in Latin music (a myriad are here), and the classic, mould-making mambos – including **Mambo Forever**, **Mambo Macoco**, **Fiesta A La King** and **Hong Kong Mambo** – remind us that Puente was forever a Mambonik.

The starting-point for these fifty tracks celebrating fifty years of music is Puente's first recording. In 1946, aged 23, Tito Rodríguez sang a bubbling, brassy rumba called ¡**Que No! ¡Que No!** The set closes on ¡**Oye Como Va!**, which carried Puente to non-Latin audiences via Carlos Santana's Latin-rock version.

"El Rey del Timbal" (King of the Timbales) was an exceptional all-rounder, a virtuoso timbales player who exploited every textural possibility of the kit (hear **Tito On Timbales**) and also a mean vibraphonist, a meticulous and inventive arranger and a dedicated band-leader. Years in the business left him with a set of showman's antics – waving drum-sticks while playing dazzling solos, grimacing and shooting mock-shock looks at the sound bursting from his drums as if he was a mere conduit for a guiding spirit (in his Afro-Cuban santería religion, he was). The joking could distract from the brilliance of his playing and the way he manipulated rows of gleaming brass and huddles of Cuban percussionists with the ease of the leader of a small, agile ensemble.

Puente leaves over a hundred albums and scores of singles covering Latin music history: the rumba-son of the opener; the cool, vibes-led bolero from the wild diva, La Lupe, on **Qué Te Pedí**; Latinized covers of American hits, including a gorgeous instrumental take on the Drifters' **On Broadway**; covers of Latin classics, including an incredible revamp of Machito's hit **Tanga**; the ultra-swinging mambos; the frenzied 1950s hit, **Ran Kan Kan**. Puente also played salsa, of course, and some of the best is served here with Johnny Pacheco, Ray Barretto, Oscar D'León, Hector Lavoe and, of course, his Queen, Celia Cruz. In the autobiographical homage **Celia And Tito**, she scats as he raises a talking-drum-like storm on timbales.

Puente had particular sensitivity with singers, including Santos Colón, on **Complicación** and **Ay Cariño**, whose rough rhythmic style carries the traditional flavour of Puerto Rico; Machito's Cuban-jazz vocalist, Graciela, youthfully playful on **El YoYo**; Miguelito Valdés in expansive mode on **Guantanaméra**; the silky Cheo Feliciano on **¡Oh! Vida**; and, at the other extreme, young 1990s star, India, who belts out **Take It Or Lose It** like a young La Lupe. But Puente's status rests on his utter mastery of rhythm. It's a talent demonstrated to perfection on this long, exhilarating album of Afro-Cuban dance.

Sue Steward

Further listening: In Session (Tropijazz) comes from Puente's super-swing super-group, the Golden Latin Jazz All Stars. Puente's **Dancemania, Vol.1** (BMC/Tropical Series) features stirring mambos in front of a wall of brass. Mongo Santamaría and Willie Bobo's **Our Man in Havana** (Fantasy) sees the ultimate conga-bongo partnership returning to Cuban roots.

68

Elis Regina

Pérolas

Som Livre, 2000

No musicians credited.

Almost twenty years after her death, reissues of Elis's greatest hits, like this CD, still have a huge market in Brazil. No other Brazilian female singer combined such talent with such a classic rock'n'roll lifestyle. Born in 1945, she shot to national stardom when she won a national television song contest in 1965, and from then until her death, in 1983, she was the unquestioned queen of Brazilian music, even through an era which saw the peak of such fine singers as Gal Costa and Maria Bethânia.

It was partly her voice, which somehow combined technical perfection – control and pitch – with an unrivalled capacity to project emotion – both happiness and pain – but it was also her chaotic, doomed life which transfixed fans. Elis only ever seemed at ease when performing; offstage, she was swindled by a succession of rapacious managers, and staggered from one disastrous love affair to another. Everything was eagerly reported by the national press, until her life seemed to resemble one of the lurid soap-operas that dominate Brazilian television. She had a suitably dramatic death – after a binge of amphetamines and alcohol in 1983 – just as she appeared to be getting herself back together. Nobody will ever know if it was suicide.

In her brief career, Elis put together the most respected repertoire of any female Brazilian singer. She was extraordinarily versatile and excelled at every genre she touched – whether samba, bossa-nova or rock. The best bossa-nova ever recorded? "Águas de Março", Elis's duet with Tom Jobim, will be on every Brazilian's list. The best samba by a woman singer? Perhaps **Mestre Sala dos Marés**, the third track on this disc. In the 1970s, Elis was the first singer that many of Brazil's finest composers – notably Tom Jobim, João Bosco and Gilberto Gil – had in mind when they wrote for others. She was easily the most sought-after live performer in Brazilian music, too, and filled venues like no-one else. The naked emotion of her singing touched a deep chord in her audiences, even when, towards the end of her life, drugs and alcohol were clearly having an impact on the quality of her singing. Her slight body, cropped hair and even, eerily, something in her voice, are reminiscent of the equally doomed, equally well-loved Edith Piaf.

Pérolas (Pearls) dates from the late 1970s, when Elis was at her peak, and gives some idea of her remarkable range. It contains samba in the shape of "Mestre Sala dos Marés"; bossa nova, in **Triste**; slow ballads, in **Aprendendo A Jogar** and **No Dia Em Que Vim Embora**; and a selection of covers of the work of most of the best songwriters of her day. A couple of songs are live recordings, and illustrate the special bond between Elis and her audience. Two live tracks in particular, **Para Lennon e McCartney** – a salute to the foreign group which had by far the most impact on Brazilian music in the 1960s – and Milton Nascimento's **Maria Maria**, were staples of her shows, their popularity heard in the roar of recognition as the first notes ring out and the audience gets to its feet. Sometimes the backing bands sound rough, especially in the more rock-influenced tracks, but Elis's fantastic voice holds it all together, articulating happiness, love and pain like no-one before or since. She is still missed.

David Cleary

Further listening: the stunning bossa nova album, **Elis e Tom** (Philips), presents all the famous Jobim hits from the early 1960s, with the vocals divided between the pair. The double CD **O Talento de Elis Regina** (Philips) takes you through the back catalogue chronologically, and includes most of the biggest hits.

69

Juan Reynoso

The Paganini of the Mexican Hot Lands

Corasón, 1993

Juan Reynoso (violin), Neyo Reynoso (guitar), Castulo Benítez de la Paz (guitar and vocals), Francisco Díaz (tamborita drum).

There are one or two albums that neither time nor technology can touch. Top of the list is this wonderful disc by an old man whose story is as remarkable as his talent. Juan Reynoso has been a *campesino* farm worker all his life. At times he and his family struggled on the edge of hunger, but Reynoso always had the solace of the violin, which he played with enormous spirit at village fiestas, parties, weddings, baptisms and any other excuse to get together with friends. As a boy he would lead local string bands (made up of two violins, one or two guitars and the small tamborita drum) in a repertoire of sones and gustos from his home region of Pungarabato, in the hot-lands of the Mexican West, along with waltzes, paso dobles and the hit tunes of the day.

In the 1950s, the heyday of Mexican music, Reynoso was invited to Mexico City to record and to play on the radio. He was only temporarily tempted to abandon the country life, however, and soon returned home. In 1972, he was recorded by a group of self-taught musicologists, and five Reynoso tunes appeared on the classic *Anthology of Mexican Sones* compilation, opening the way for Reynoso to receive the much-deserved reputation he now enjoys. This 1994 collection pays exclusive homage to the great violinist.

El Paganini de la Tierra Caliente (The Paganini of the

Hot Lands) built on this reputation, and its reception was surprisingly warm in the capital, where Mexico's enormous wealth of traditional music had been mostly ignored. Although it didn't make the best-seller lists, the album was heard by television producers, festival organizers and even presidential advisers, and Reynoso was invited to record, travel and give concerts and interviews – and even received a prestigious cultural award from the hands of the President himself, Ernesto Zedillo. Reynoso confessed that the best part of the prize was the money that accompanied it, and admitted that he preferred to play music than answer questions or sit for photos.

This disc has the feel of the greatest Irish traditional fiddlers: the playing is passionate, direct and soulful, and Don Juan's violin simply soars in the complex improvised flourishes with which he embellishes the traditional pieces. The soaring **Son Guerrerense** lets loose some incredible violin solos, revealing exactly why Reynoso is the undisputed master of the instrument in Mexico. The simpler gusto, **La Tortolita**, which also features his voice – full of soul but without the virtuosity of his violin-playing – is a song about the perils facing a little sparrow who knocks at the window because he wants to come into the safety of the room. As in many sones, animals are used as metaphors for human relationships. **El Jilguerito** is an instrumental son, while **La Rema** is a sweeter, simpler affair.

Fortune has not treated Reynoso as poorly as it has most Mexican traditional musicians; now aged 84, he continues to perform. He tells the story of how his son gave him a second-hand violin twenty years ago, apologizing for not having money to buy a new one. Don Juan didn't mind because the violin had a good sound, he told him. Those permitted to examine the label inside the instrument will, he claims, discover that the "Paganini of the Hot Lands" is playing a Stradivarius.

Mary Farquharson

Further listening: Los Camperos de Valles's **El Triunfo** (Discos Corasón), features Reynoso's rival, Heliododo Copadom, who plays a majestic country violin with a similar blend of technical prowess and exuberance of spirit.

70

Ismael Rivera

El Sonero Mayor

WS Latino/ Sony, 1999

Ismael Rivera (vocals), Rafael Cortijo (percussion, leader), Rafael Ithier (piano),
Roberto Roena (bongos), Martín Quiñones (congas), Miguel Cruz (bass), Kito Vélez,
Victor Pérez (trumpet), Eddie Pérez, Hector Santos (sax).

When Puerto Rican singer Ismael Rivera died, in 1987, the whole island went into mourning and the narrow street where he had lived became a site of pilgrimage. "Maelo", as he was universally known, was one of the greatest and most loved singers the island had known. Cuban icon Beny Moré nicknamed him "El Sonero Mayor" (The Greatest Singer).
His songs – many, like those on this fabulous compilation, first recorded nearly fifty years ago – are still performed today.

The handsome singer was an important figurehead for the country's black population. With the bandleader and percussionist Rafael Cortijo, he adopted the traditional Afro-Rican bomba and plena styles and dressed them for the city, adapting them to a band alive with saxophones and trumpets and powered by Cuban percussion. Bomba's drumming, singing and dancing is closely related to Cuban rumba, while the lighter, more gossipy plena is resonant of Trinidadian calypso, the melodies carried on guitars.

This compilation represents the peak era of Cortijo's Combo, from 1955 to 1959, when they performed live most days on the television *Show del Mediodía*. The pair first sang together in dodgy bars in the port of San Juan before moving into more mainstream entertainment – Rivera's first professional job, aged twenty, was singing at a tourist hotel. In 1955, they released **El**

Bombón de Elena, and overnight it was jumping out of every jukebox in the capital. They looked like country cousins in the explosive New York Latin music scene but the song caused a sensation, with its fast, jumpy plena rhythm. It opens to the stirring rhythmic call of a pandereta – the large frame drum typical of plena – and uses the Cuban "old-lady voices" style as its central chorus. It is rough and ready, and effortlessly danceable, with sophisticated big-band saxophone breaks. Maelo is casual, his words slurred, his husky voice quintessentially Puerto Rican.

Rivera was a superb improviser. In **Monta Mi Caballito**, he tries to get a girl onto his father's "uneducated" mule (suggested by braying trumpets) and chants fast, tongue-twisting rhymes – the mark of the true *salsero*. The scorchingly catchy **El Negro Bembón –** about a handsome man who is loved (and hassled) by everyone – comes closest to modern salsa, a cowbell clanging out its beat over Rafael Ithier's sensual piano.

Bombas were the mainstay of Ismael Rivera's repertoire; even that Costa del Sol anthem, **Volare**, gets the bouncing bomba treatment. The hissing slash of the wooden güiro is central to their sound – in **Besito de Coco** (Little Coconut Kiss) it emits streams of kisses. The brassy, Cuban **Cucala, Cucala** – also a huge hit for Celia Cruz – is, in Cortijo's hands, a riot of trumpet choruses and fast vocals, driven by its lurching beat. Cortijo's **El Chivo De La Campana** has a calypso lilt, with Ismael in top form and his young pianist in jazz-inspired mood. Ithier is also prominent on **¡Ahí Na Ma!**, where trumpets shout across to each other as he spars with the percussion.

In 1962, Rafael Ithier led a breakaway from Cortijo's Combo and founded El Gran Combo, another of Puerto Rico's national treasures. Maelo, on the other hand, went to jail on a drugs charge. The moment had passed.

Sue Steward

Further listening: Rafael Cortijo's exciting **Time Machine** (Musical Productions) merged prog rock with salsa, adding Caribbean elements for good measure. **Roberto Roena y su Apollo Sound's 5** (Fania) features the legendary band in their early-1980s rough and rocking salsa heyday.

71

Virgínia Rodrigues

Nós (Us)

Hannibal, 2000

Virgínia Rodrigues (vocals), Caetano Veloso (vocals), Celso Fonseca (guitar, calimba), Ramiro Musotto (percussion, berimbau), Robertinho Silva (percussion), plus winds and strings.

When Virgínia Rodrigues appeared at London's Albert Hall in the summer of 2000, she was the least familiar singer on a stage packed with legends from the tropicália and samba era. Every song drew cheers from the audience. But the reserved Afro-Brazilian woman with the snakey braided hair and voluminous African print dress stood apart from the others, looking more like a gospel singer than a bossa diva. When the spotlight turned on her, her first notes transformed the occasion from a high-spirited, sexy dance party into a religious experience. Rodrigues's pure, high-contralto voice soared around the room, rolling against the gilded interior of the dome like golden brandy inside a warmed glass.

In 1994, Caetano Veloso was visiting Salvador de Bahia, his home town in northeast Brazil, when he saw Rodrigues singing with the drum group, Olodum. He was so smitten by her voice that he asked to record her. In their first album together, *Sol Negro*, she sang to a cocktail of Brazilian styles, but this second album, **Nós**, is a more thought-out concept. Songs were chosen to suit Rodrigues's extraordinary voice, and to reflect her involvement with the music of Afro-Brazilian religion, candomblé, including chants, hymns and praise songs to the deities.

The measured, dignified album opens with a startling, minute-long chant, **Canto Para Exú**, which leads into **Uma História de Ifá**, a song about candomblé's original home in the ancient Yoruba city of Elijibo (in what is now Nigeria). **Ojú Obá**, with its spikey guitars and violin accompaniment, tells of the arrival of a deity in the midst of worshippers, but could be easily mistaken for a passionate reunion of the flesh. **Mimar Você** is an unambiguous plea to a human lover, an exquisitely slow song, accompanied by a cello and violins. Rodrigues's voice is open and sustained, and soars to high, clear notes of ecstasy.

Throughout the album, Afro-Brazilian percussion, rhythms and religious chants are fused seamlessly with guitars, saxophones, brass and chamber strings, and the slow viola and cello accompaniments seem designed for her voice. Which is exceptional – resonant, pure and almost ecclesiastical. This incredible album contains many sublime moments. The duet between Rodrigues and Veloso on **Jeito Faceiro** opens with the sound of trickling waters played on Celo Fonseca's carimba (thumb piano), flowing through the song against a poignant solo violin. Veloso drops his voice to a suitably devotional pitch and the harmonies of the two singers take on a devotional quality.

The outstanding **Afrêketê** is the album's most catchy, upbeat song, driven at a choppy, near-ska percussive rhythm. With its melodic, swing-era saxophone phrases, it's a compelling dance tune. The singer's key changes every few lines add to the rich emotional appeal in the telling of a familiar scene: "The city of Salvador awoke in the morning, playing bells, and the Afrêketê bloque arrived carrying a small saint". In a new incarnation, the heavily percussive song **Male Debalê** was pulled from its religious context, and treated to a re-mix by London DJ, where it hit the city's World Dance scene.

Sue Steward

Further listening: The drums on Paul Simon's album with Grupo Cultural Olodum, **Rhythm of the Saints** (Warner Brothers), were recorded live in the main square of Salvador de Bahia; Simon injects his own lyrical magic to create a joyful celebration of Bahia style. **Beleza Tropical 2: Novo! Mais! Melhor!** (Luaka Bop) brings together the range of Bahia sounds.

72

Arsenio Rodríguez

Arsenio Rodríguez

Artex/Egrem, 1993

Arsenio Rodríguez (composer, tres guitar, leader), Luis "Lili" Martínez (piano), Marcelina Guerra (guitar), Félix Chapottín (lead trumpet), Miguelito Cuní (vocals), Nilo Alfonso (bass), Antonio Suárez (bongos), Israel Rodríguez (congas); plus Chucho Valdés, Grupo Irakere and Grupo Manguaré.

"El Ciego Maravilloso" (The Blind Marvel), Arsenio Rodríguez, was one of the major Cuban influences on salsa. Ignacio Arsenio Travieso Scull was born in 1911, in an African neighbourhood of Matanzas. The grandson of a slave, he grew up immersed in the music and customs of the people of the Congo. His first musical experiences were playing percussion, but in 1926, aged fifteen and already blind, he took up the resonant, six-stringed (three doubles) tres guitar, the leading melody voice in the Cuban style called son.

Arsenio moved to Havana in 1930, where he joined Orquesta Casino de la Playa, whose singer, Miguelito Valdés, first popularised his compositions. In spite of their central musical roles, during the shows he and the other dark-skinned musicians were frequently made to play behind screens to avoid offending white audiences. In 1940, Arsenio formed his "Conjunto"; they performed at the beer gardens of El Tropical, where hip young Afro-Cubans danced to his revolutionary new sound. The eight-piece son unit featured a wind section with an extra trumpet (the soloist was the sensational, high-blowing Félix Chapottín), a conga drum beside the bongos and a piano (the visionary Lili Martínez). The conjunto allowed space for solos and the resulting sound was louder, broader and deeper than son had ever achieved before. In 1950, Arsenio moved to New York, just as mambo, which he helped invent, was making waves.

This collection includes three tribute versions of Arsenio hits, opening with a florid, impressionist homage by pianist Chucho Valdés. Irakere's **Dile A Catalina**, from their 1980s period, reveals the extraordinary evolution of son, while Grupo Manguaré's **Hecheros Pa' Un Palo** sticks close to the original and showcases today's virtuoso *tresero* (tres guitarist), Pancho Amat. The rest is sheer Arsenio magic.

Buenavista En Guagancó introduces the fabulous, warbling falsetto of Miguelito Cuní. The opening tres and percussion dialogue on **Fiesta En El Solar** plunges deep into the African roots of rumba – a shuffling, trance-like rhythm backs the breathless tres solo. Arsenio held the instrument under his chin, his face impassive, his unseeing eyes behind dark glasses. He was no delicate finger-picker, but played forcefully and emotionally. By the time of this hit, an electric pick-up lent a strident, bluesy edge to the notes. **Juventud Amaliana** takes son onto the dance floor, trumpets driving the melody while Miguelito Cuní's operatic tenor shoots off into falsetto, proving why he was so adored.

The tres carries the catchy cha-cha-cha rhythm on **Blanca Paloma**, with the güiro smooching alongside. **Bésame Aquí** is slower and more hypnotic, the singers switching between solo and unison, according to cha-cha convention. The erotic games in **Mami Me Gustó** – "this thing you're doing to me, baby, I like it" – were years ahead of "salsa erotica". The trumpeters emit shuddery orgasmic choruses as Cuní's voice rises and falls, and Arsenio's sharper, more electric tone pre-empts Jimi Hendrix.

Sue Steward

Further listening: Latin New York pianist Larry Harlow recorded the classic **Tribute to Arsenio Rodríguez** (Fania/Sonido) just months after Arsenio's death. Rodríguez's influence can be heard in the music of guitarist Manuel Galbán, who led 1960s pop group Los Zafiros into the Cuban charts – try **Bossa Cubana** by Los Zafiros (World Circuit).

Silvio Rodríguez

Canciones Urgentes

Luaka Bop, 1991/2000

Silvio Rodríguez (vocals, guitar), Grupo Afrocuba, Orchestra EGREM.

Silvio Rodríguez is a modern troubadour. He began writing love songs with a simple guitar accompaniment in the 1960s and in doing so forged an entirely new approach to the Cuban romantic song. He used it to express doubt and vulnerability as well as the feeling of love itself. In the 1980s and 1990s, Rodríguez emerged as one of the most influential South American songwriters and became famous throughout the Spanish speaking world. His genius is his knack of using beautiful melodies to tell thought-provoking stories.

When he and his contemporary, Pablo Milanés, began their musical careers in Cuba, in the 1960s, they encountered problems as their bohemian, rock-influenced attitudes challenged the dogmatic expression of Revolutionary culture then holding sway in Cuba. But their talent and tenacity led them to be invited to become part of ICAIC (the Cuban Cinematographic Institute), where they were invited to form a co-operative, Grupo de Experimentación Sonora (Experimental Sound Group), composing film soundtracks. From the mid 1980s until the early 1990s, Rodríguez performed and recorded with Cuban jazz-rock band Grupo Afrocuba, whose musical director, Oriente López, arranged many of his songs for the big band format. The tracks on this record are accompanied by both Afrocuba and the EGREM studio orchestra based in Havana.

The album opens on an essential Rodríguez theme, the dream

– although **Sueño de Una Noche de Verano** is actually a nightmare of war and violence. **Sueño con Serpientes** begins with a quote from Bertolt Brecht and carries a message to persevere in life's struggle. **Unicornio**, a metaphor for dreams and ideals, is a tender song about a lost blue unicorn, and testimony to Rodríguez's belief that "fantasy is necessary in order to live". The song captivated young audiences throughout the Americas and there were numerous reported sightings of the unicorn, most poignantly by freedom fighters in El Salvador.

Questioning belief is a constant Rodríguez theme and represented here in several songs. **Causas y Azares** (Causes and Fate) was the key opening song all through his mammoth 1989 tour of Cuba that celebrated the thirtieth anniversary of the Revolution. The equally upbeat **La Maza** (The Hammer) begins deceptively with an intimate guitar; Rodríguez's vulnerable-as-a-feather voice belies his passionate lyrics about believing in life while embracing all its contradictions. **Canto Arena** (I Sing Of Sand), with its musical references to The Beatles, asserts belief in life while musing on the fragmentary nature of existence: "I sing of sand, of rock that becomes multitudinous in clear water." **Canción Urgente Para Nicaragua** (Urgent Song For Nicaragua) sets the briefly successful Sandinista revolutionary struggle in the context of the history of the Americas.

But it's not all politics and revolution. The buoyant and joyful **Como Esperando Abril** features a brilliantly improvised jazz piano finale. The song's complex, open-ended nature is typical of Rodríguez, as is the sheer joy it expresses in living and loving – themes echoed in **Nuestro Tema**. The album ends with **O Melancolía**, Rodriguez's serenade to Melancholy, a gentle piano supporting his husky voice.

Jan Fairley

Further listening: The title song of Pablo Milanés's **Días de Gloria** (Universal Music, Spain/Mexico) can be seen as an epitaph for the ideals of the Revolution: "The days of glory flew by and only the memory is left". Try Carlos Varela's **En Vivo** (Discmedia, Spain) and **Monedas Al Aire** (Qbadisc) for a taste of the more outspoken, rock-influenced generation.

Compay Segundo

Lo Mejor de la Vida

East-West/Warner Music, 1998

Compay Segundo (armonico guitar, second voice), Hugo Garzón (lead voice), Benito Suárez (guitar), Pedrito Ibáñez (guitar), Cotó (tres), Barbarito Torres (laúd), Raimundo Amador (flamenco guitar), Salvador Repilado (double bass); Omara Portuondo, Silvio Rodríguez, Pío Leyva, Félix Valoy, Martirio (guest vocals), and others.

Few people reading this book will be unfamiliar with the fairy-story of Cuban guitarist and singer Compay Segundo. His smiling face under a rakish white panama, cigar clamped between his teeth or burning in long bony fingers as he plucks an old customized guitar – Francisco Repilado, as he is officially named, cuts an unmistakable figure. His sprightly, sexy little shuffles and gravelly voice were perpetual delights on the film and album of *Buena Vista Social Club*. At the age of 89, a year after the album took off, he toured Europe with the energy and enthusiasm of a young rock pup. Today his modest home on Calle Salud boasts a Grammy award, files of press cuttings and a wardrobe of smart new clothes – a dramatic change of fortune for a retired cigar-roller whose heyday was half a century earlier. Since *BVSC*, Compay Segundo has been prolific, but **Lo Mejor de la Vida** (The Best In Life) is exceptional. The opening **El Camisón de Pepa** (Pepa's Nightshirt) was a cheeky hit in 1927 for Compay's friend, Antonio Machín, and is reproduced as classic acoustic son buoyed by bubbling congas and bongos. It showcases Compay's distinctive armonico guitar (a customized seven-string instrument), plucked harmonies cascading in sparkling droplets while Benito Suárez plies a more conventional solo.

One theme running throughout the record is the musical relationship between Spain and Cuba, a fascination for the old man since his first visit to Spain in the late 1990s. **Cuba y España** celebrates the links between his repertoire of Cuba's most Spanish song styles – the guitar-based punto guajiro, guaracha and son – and their ancestral forms in Europe, and features a distinctively Andalucian quality in the accompanying Cuban lute (laúd) of Barbarito Torres. **Es Mejor Vivir Así** is a dramatic bolero duet engaging Compay's gritty baritone with the warbling heights of the flamenco diva Martirio. He instructed her to "cry this bolero with me" and the result is utterly winning, as their contrasting voices rise and swell, meet and part like smoke from two gypsy fires. **Juliancito (Tu Novia de Botó)** sees Ramón Amador's Andalucian guitar and high vocals added to the session with Martirio – a Cuban flamenco delight.

Back home in Havana, Compay invited two familiar Buena Vista Club members, Omara Portuondo and Pío Leyva, on board. He called up Félix Valoy's wonderfully, wilfully wild and operatic tenor for **Frutas del Caney**, as well as Cuba's leading folk singer Silvio Rodríguez, who takes a disappointingly background role to Compay's close-miked lead vocals in **Fidelidad**. Compay's duets with the fruity voice of Pío Leyva, **La Ternera** and **La Juma de Ayer**, are particularly poignant, as the two men's voices have teased each other for over fifty years.

In places the nonagenarian can be forgiven for losing pitch or slipping behind his partner; it seems to add to the sentiment of the lyrics. The marvellous closing number, **Son de Negros en Cuba**, is the guitarist's musical adaptation of Federico García Lorca's 1920s ode to the African son that had entranced him during a visit to Santiago de Cuba – where Compay was then performing. The band plays it as the poet would have heard it – a perfect union of Spanish and African music.

Sue Steward

Further listening: The early quartet work of Antonio Machín (who also had great success in Spain) is brilliantly captured on **Cuarteto Machín 1935–1939** (Harlequin).

Sidestepper

More Grip

Palm Pictures, 2000

Richard Blair (producer), Iván Benavides (vocals, producer), Teto Ocampo (guitar), Orbe Ortiz (tiple), Juan Carlos "El Chato" Rivas (bass), Roberto Cuao (timbales, güiro), Luis Pacheco (congas), and others.

Richard Blair got his break as a producer – in England – with the Colombian singer-songwriter Totó La Momposina in 1991, and was smitten by her joyful Latin repertoire. He took up an invitation to visit her communal musicians' house in Bogotá and stayed for three years, immersed in classic salsa from New York, Cuba and Colombia, as well as Totó's own folk songs, while vinyl from London and Kingston, Jamaica kept him abreast of the burgeoning revolutions in drum'n'bass and reggae. In 1995, with singer Carlos Vives, he produced "La Tierra del Olvido", an album of Columbian vallenato – it won a Grammy – and met the band's bassist, Iván Benavides, who would be his future partner in the fusion project known as Sidestepper.

Blair's first experiments in fitting Latin rhythms and instruments to drum'n'bass beats and samples created the album *Southern Star* (1997) and the cult single "Logozo" in 1998. By that time, Benavides was running a punkish electric folk band called Bloque, with Sidestepper on the side. But the album **More Grip**, and its spin-off boogaloo hip-hop single, **Hoy Tenemos (Right Now!)**, would put the band on the world map.

The two producers rounded up musicians from Bogotá's new wave scene and recorded these ten songs, built around an assortment of upbeat Latin rhythms – including mambo, rumba, cha-cha-cha and boogaloo – and treated to an assortment of dance producers' electronic tricks and sampling wizardry. Halfway through "Hoy Tenemos", Blair and Benavides pare the track down from the full horn, percussion and vocal free-for-all to a spacey dub, then build it up again. They employ the same technique on **Chevere Chevere,** which is otherwise full-tilt 1970s-era New York salsa, updated by Sergio Arias's Spanish rap.

Catholic taste and a sophisticated understanding of a wide range of music results in a confident mix-and-match feel running right through the album. It even trawls the English-speaking Caribbean for inspiration. The gorgeous **Linda Manigua** features a husky samba-esque duet between Andrea Echevarri and Johana Marín, working in Latin-ska mode at a brisk skanking pace created by the timbales beats. Gustavo "the Panther" García completes the mood with dramatically authentic ska trombone choruses.

The more authentic Latin tracks range from the demented Pérez Prado-era mambo of **Side Stepper**, with its old-fashioned horns and convincing Prado-style grunts, to the serene charanga of **Me Muero**. But even within one song, the mood and terrain may change: "Chevere Chevere", for instance, switches suddenly from the flute-and-violin elegance of charanga, as singer Ronald Infante adopts the deep, bluesy tone of a country son singer.

From being an ad hoc studio band, Sidestepper graduated, in 2000, to touring as a full group. After a successful European debut they returned to their home city to be met by delighted club-goers. For Bogotanos, **La Bara** (slang for a joint) is the album's winner, for its compulsive reggae beat, Mick Ball's raging trumpet solo, Teto Ocampo's rock guitar rumblings and the chorus of "Pass it to me!" .

Sue Steward

Further listening: Discoteca: firin´ Latino house, funk electro and disco (Ocho) compiles salsa fusions from the 1970s to the present, and puts Sidestepper in their dance-fusion context. **La Línea: Future Latin Beats** (Manteca) brings together Latin, hip-hop, house, funk and drum 'n' bass and points to the exciting future of Latin dance.

76

La Sonora Ponceña

On The Right Track

Inca/Sonido, 1988

Enrique "Quique" Lucca (leader), Enrique "Papo" Lucca (piano, flugel horn, keyboards), Delfín Pérez, Ramon A. Rodríguez, Ángel Velez, Alfredo del Valle (trumpet), Vicente "Little Johnny" Rivero (congas), and others.

One of salsa's most superlative bands, La Sonora Ponceña started out in 1944 as Orquesta Internacional, a two-trumpet outfit performing Cuban-style hits; director Enrique "Quique" Lucca expanded and renamed the big band in 1954. Since then, he has watched it mature into a full-size powerhouse of salsa with its own unique and distinctively polished sound – an institution now truly the Sound of *all* Puerto Rico.

In 1968, "Quique" handed over to his son "Papo", a piano prodigy who had joined in 1954 – he began the transformation of the band's musical "voice". He created a sophisticated mosaic from a weave of four trumpets, with three vocalists employing Afro-Cuban call-and-response, doowop, jazz harmonies and scatting styles, and light-fingered Afro-Cuban percussion playing sensual rather than funky rhythms. The effect is smoother and slower than the brasher, more Afro-sound of mainland-based salsa. Papo's ringing, jazzy piano is a focus throughout, injecting an irresistible swing.

As the group perfected their sound through the 1970s and 1980s, gathering awards for every album released, Papo's other job with the Fania All Stars in New York helped spread Ponceña's popularity. This album represents Ponceña at its peak, even though it had by then lost the gloriously wrought vocals of

Yolanda Rivera. The band's secret weapons – trumpeters Delfín Pérez ("El del Café"), Ramon A. Rodríguez ("El Cordobés"), Ángel Velez ("Pocholo") and Alfredo del Valle ("Freddie") – were, like Papo Lucca, veterans, and their consistency contributed to the orchestra's burnished sound.

The nine songs of **On the Right Track** acknowledge Papo's attraction to new Cuban music – a risky admission in many Miami circles in the late 1980s, where contact with Cuba could result in blackballing by anti-Castro fanatics. **La Rumba Soy Yo** uses the saoco rhythm to tell the story of Afro-Cuban rumba, with a fiery conga solo by then up-and-coming young virtuoso Giovanni Hidalgo. **Sigo Pensando En Ti** is a gorgeous love song by Cuban nueva canción icon, Pablo Milanés. Papo transformed the simple original into a sashaying salsa number, tailored to the twirling Puerto Rican dance style. Opening to a flush of trumpets, it uses synthesized vibes behind the husky vocals. The trumpet arrangements are breath-taking – flaring, fanning, erupting in spiky solos or braying in unison.

In continental mood, **A Cali** acknowledges the entry into mainstream salsa of bands from Colombia's salsa capital, Cali. It is a compelling dance track, moving to that jumpy, poppy, saoco beat ("the witches' rhythm") so adored by Colombian dancers. **Franqueza Cruel**, by the "Gershwin of Puerto Rican salsa", Tite "Curet" Alonso, charts the end of an affair. It develops from a minimalistic doowop chorus, backed by echoey piano, into a softly flowing rhythm. The highlight is Papo's formidable style – left hand locked onto a rocking Cuban clave rhythm while the right rolls around glorious jazz chords. **Abanacue** is pure Ponceña, a song about Cuban son (the basis of their music) and yet another showcase of Papo's inventiveness.

Sue Steward

Further listening: La Sonora Ponceña's **Determination** (Inca/Sonido) is the album of choice for the stirring voice of Yolanda Rivera. Mulenze's **De Regreso** (NRT) marks a fantastic return to form by a very under-rated Puerto Rican band who, like Sonora Ponceña, are not afraid to use class jazz phrasing and harmonies. This is highly sophisticated, modern salsa.

77

Mercedes Sosa

30 Años

Polygram, 1993

No musicians credited.

"Magnificent Mercedes", "The Voice of Latin America", Argentine singer Mercedes Sosa doesn't perform her own material but completely and unequivocally makes the songs she sings her own. **30 Años** (Thirty Years) celebrates Sosa through her own choice of material, and acts as a history of Latin America's nueva canción movement, offering, as it does, key songs by key songwriters that captured vital moments in the emotional history of the Americas.

The record kicks off momentously with **La Maza**, by Cuban songwriter Silvio Rodríguez, whose writing also features in **Unicornio**, a wistfully idealistic story that led a generation throughout the continent to embroider the lost unicorn of the song on their T-shirts. The poignant **Todo Cambia**, by Chilean Julio Numhauser, is a passionate song of exile. A live performance of **Sólo le Pido a Dios**, written by Argentine folk-rock singer, León Gieco, recalls the song's significance to the peace movement during the Falklands war. It kept alive the spirit of young Argentines sent unwillingly to war. Gieco's presence as second voice and harmonica-player, and the audience's choruses, makes this song historic. That courageous mood is maintained in a duet with Antonio Tarragó Ros on his tender **María Va**, and on Sosa's lovely version of **Canción Para Carito**.

A live duet with Horacio Guarany, the composer of the deeply Argentine piece, **Si Se Calla El Cantor** (If The Singer Is

Silenced) is a powerful testament to the political commitment of nueva canción's radical generation of musicians. It is followed by Sosa's emotionally exhilarating version of rock star Charly García's **Inconsciente Colectivo**. The combination of Sosa's rootsy approach to the song, coupled with the vulnerable edge of Milton Nascimento's and García's wild tones in such a breathtaking song of freedom and dreams (it was first popular during the Falklands period) is nothing short of superb. **Canción Con Todos** (Song with Everyone), regarded by many as the hymn of the Americas, is often sung at the end of song festivals; it is a wonderfully understated piece, despite its message of pluralistic unity. There is a dramatic shift of mood with **Años**, by Cuban songwriter Pablo Milanés, in which Sosa's voice caresses the author's reflections on memory and the passing of time and love.

Mercedes Sosa's dynamic remaking of Argentine folk music is particularly evident on **Alfonsina y el Mar** and the gaucho song, **La Arenosa**. Her version of Atahualpa Yupanqui's arrangement of the Caribbean lullaby **Duerme Negrito**, and his beautiful **Luna Tucumana** (Tucumán Moon), celebrate the fact that they shared Tucumán as a childhood home.

Sadly, the compilation notes fail to provide details of the musicians who play on this CD and so it is impossible to heap upon them the praise they deserve. The presiding sound – of subtle guitar, bass and drum kit with bombo drum and Andean percussion – suggests it is the ensemble she worked with during most of the 1980s and 1990s. Sosa's glorious voice in all its many emotional shadings brings them and a brilliant galaxy of composers into full focus in the final song, the bittersweet, **Dale Alegría a Mi Corazón** (Bring Happiness to My Heart), which alone makes this disc covetable.

Jan Fairley

Further listening: folk-rock hero León Gieco has accompanied Mercedes on many occasions and is a huge star in his own right, as heard on **Lo Mejor, Pensar En Nada, Cada Día, Somos Más, Soy Un Pobre Agujero** (Orfeon). Of the next generation, the talented Soledad shares Mercedes's vocal force and charisma, heard on **Yo Sí Quiero A Mi País** (Sony).

78

Yma Sumac

Mambo! And More

Rev-Ola/Creation Records, 1997

No musicians credited.

The extraordinary Peruvian singer Yma Sumac claimed, somewhat controversially, to be descended from an Inca princess and to have grown up in a small Andean village inhabited by Quechua Indians. That autobiography certainly tallies with her subsequent image.

The young Sumac was spotted singing in festivals in Peru, and rapidly graduated to a radio station in Buenos Aires, where her incredible five-octave voice caused a sensation. In 1947, aged twenty, she moved to Los Angeles and, within three years, had a number one with the exotic "Voice of the Xtaby". After that, Hollywood was her oyster. She arrived just as stateside Americans were beginning their love affair with Latin music, and the charts were crowded with mambos, sambas and cha-cha-chas by the likes of Xavier Cugat and Carmen Miranda. The Brazilian Miranda was on a roll – squealing, crooning and chirping her way through US films and hit albums – and Yma found a niche beside her.

In Hollywood she met the composer and record producer Moises Vivanco, who adored her uninhibited vocal pyrotechnics and brilliant range. Vivanco – an extreme eclectic with a kitsch passion for "Latin exotica" – became her manager, producer and husband. This exhilarating compilation features some of their greatest songs, plus several previously unreleased tracks by Vivanco's whacky orchestra. The songs reinforce Yma's wonderfully confused and completely inauthentic "Latin diva" image.

She posed for record sleeves against bamboo curtains, parrots and Inca sculptures, wearing embroidered robes and gold jewellery. Vivanco provided a fabulous musical collage to match.

Yma never conformed to a conventional narrative song, and rarely got further than a few phrases before soaring to the musical heights, or breaking into scatting. Her voice has many identities and she wears them all within a few bars. She conjures birdsong at dawn in open-throated warbling in **Taki Rari**, then swoops and lunges like an Andean bird of prey. Her scatting is more offbeat than Ella's, and never so refined. She sings in guttural Peruvian Spanish on the deliciously kitsch feast concocted from Xavier Cugat's hit **Babalou** – enlivened by flute, clarinet, Chinese drums and Spanish guitar. She uses indecipherable words – maybe Quechua or imagined Inca – on the magnificent **Gopher**, on which she rises from deep masculine grunts accompanied by a shrill, braying trumpet chorus, to pure thin-air heights where her famous warbling vibrato never falters.

The musical backing includes mambos and cha-chas, flamenco and pastiches of Latin American Indian idioms. On **Cha Cha Gitano**, Vivanco creates a collage from strings and flamenco guitars against her dramatic, Andalucian singing. A touch of the panpipes pervades **Huachachina**, where Yma's untranslatable crooning is chased by a fast-picked guitar, pre-Columbian maracas, a fairground organ and a piano.

In the late 1980s, the elderly Sumac emerged from retirement for a handful of US gigs, performing on a set decorated with a ruined "Inca" temple. Her voice had narrowed by an octave or more, but that still left more scope than most singers are born with. Any doubts about her authenticity were quickly banished as she transfixed audiences once again with her Andean magic.

Sue Steward

Further listening: Carmen Miranda, 1930–1945 (Harlequin/Interstate) features 25 songs from the fabulously over-the-top Brazilian singer, too often remembered only for her fruity head-dresses. **The Songs of Pedro Almodóvar** (EMI) reveals the cult director's camp good taste in soundtracks, and adds his own songs with flamenco singer McNamara.

79

Los Tigres del Norte

Corridos Prohibidos

Fonovisa, circa 1984

Jorge Hernández (vocals, accordion), Eduardo Hernández (sax, chorus), Hernán Hernández (bass, chorus), Oscar Lara (drums), Luis Hernández (bao sexto guitar), Guadalupe Olivo (sax).

Far from being the most recent recording by Los Tigres del Norte, this collection of corrido ballads was released in the mid 1980s – but it was the one which finally opened doors for a group that has since become a Mexican institution. The band members have starred in twenty films, won several Grammys and are one of the few commercial bands that dare to criticize the government – and they manage to get away with it.

As their name suggests, Los Tigres del Norte originate in the north of Mexico, in the state of Sinaloa – famous for good polka music, drug trafficking and exploitative fruit farms. The four Hernández brothers, plus a cousin and a friend, first got together thirty years ago as a local band singing corrido ballads about local anti-heroes. They rode in on a contemporary version of music that dates back to the nineteenth century: south of the border this style of music is called norteño, and is immensely popular, while in the States it is called Tex-Mex and has a smaller audience – the commercial hits are blander ballads. Fans of Flaco Jiménez will recognise the bouncy, rustic, accordion-led style, though the emphasis is on the songs rather than supercharged accordion playing. In the Mexico of today, Los Tigres's corridos are a popular alternative to distorted news reports.

By the mid 1980s, Los Tigres were enormously popular on both sides of Mexico's northern border. Their rhinestone-cowboy image and real-life lyrics conflicted with the white-bread, factory-polished pop promoted by Mexico's all-powerful Televisa entertainment empire, but the huge success of **Corridos Prohibidos** (Banned Corridos) led them to reconsider; Televisa bought the rights to this recording, the last before Los Tigres hit national superstardom. They now fill the biggest football stadiums, travel in a fleet of coaches and have a separate truck for the cowboy costumes that are as elaborate as their music is simple.

The songs on this disc, like the corrido genre itself, are simple, affairs sung in nasal tones – they lack the intensity of highly syncopated and improvised styles such as traditional Mexican son. But few corridos rival **El Gato Félix**, a ballad about an outspoken journalist who refuses to remain silent, and pays for his valour with his life, or **La Camioneta Gris**, the story of a pair of *narcos* (drug runners) shot by the police on the way back from honeymooning in Acapulco.

The group's success opened the way for a boom in norteño and banda music. Six-piece bands like Los Tigres and eighteen-piece wind bands like the Recodo play polkas, cumbias and the latest hit songs to an avid public that can't get enough of high-energy dances like the *quebradita*, or "little back-breaker", which involves some testing steps. Despite their newfound commercial success, Los Tigres seem to have their feet on the ground. They continue to sing in a matter-of-fact way about corruption, smuggling and shooting and, true to life, their anti-heroes are also vulnerable. In **Fox Of Ojinaga**, they sing: "The slyest fox can be trapped with the collaboration of his own folks" – and this was long before Mexico elected a President called Vicente Fox, who would need eyes in the back of his head.

Mary Farquharson

Further listening: El Acordeón de Oro (Harmony/Sony) features great playing from Los Bravos del Norte, a long-established commercial norteño band. **Corridos Zapatistas** (INAH) is a beautifully presented disc of corridos and related genres from central Mexico.

80

Felipe Urbán y su Danzonera

Aniversario – 15 Éxitos, Vol. III

Titanio Records, 2001

Felipe Urbán (trombone), Jose Urbán (alto sax), Juventino Motolinia (alto sax),
Margarito González (tenor sax), Jorge Gazca (baritone sax), Agustín Urbán (trumpet),
Roberto Mendoza (trumpet), Apolo Martínez (violin), Raul Urbán (Timbales), Eleodoro
Urbán (güiro), Valentín Martínez (piano), Ediberto López (bass).

Although Greatest Hits compilations are usually limited to artists with an arsenal of recordings behind them, this is not the case with the wonderful danzón orchestra run by Felipe Urbán. A legend on the Mexico City dance-hall scene for nearly thirty years, this very Mexican big band has such an enormous following that its fans eventually demanded that the music they had only heard on stage be recorded. It took five volumes to squeeze on the most requested numbers alone. Volume Three, **Aniversario**, offers straight danzones, many of them composed by Urbán himself, as well as his arrangements of well-known classics.

One of the first dance crazes to come out of Cuba, danzón arrived in Mexico in the late nineteenth century. It was first performed live by Cuban orchestras and later penetrated into the country through recordings made in Havana, reaching its heyday in the 1930s and 1940s. The Mexican danzón developed along its own route and has become more melodramatic, less virtuosic – and vastly more popular than the Cuban version. Every day of the week, six or seven top *danzoneras* (danzón orchestras) fill Mexico City's three legendary vast dance halls: the Los Angeles, the California and the Colonia. The music, like the two-tone patent leather shoes and starched shirts of the male dancers, is certainly elegant. But this is not a nostalgic scene – in Mexico danzón has simply never gone out of fashion.

The crowds of two or three thousand who traditionally accompany Felipe Urbán every Tuesday evening at the Los Angeles are there exclusively to dance. To this highly discerning public, Felipe Urbán is the master. His band was formed in 1972 and, while it is not the oldest orchestra, the combination of its musicianship with Urbán's compositions and arrangements has proved a great success. In recent years, Felipe has played the hallowed Bellas Artes Palace in Mexico City, and even led the band that welcomed the Pope to Mexico City.

The line-up of the thirteen-piece danzón orchestra relies heavily on trombone, trumpet, sax and clarinet, and includes a single violin alongside the piano, with timbales as the vital percussion ingredient. In the dance hall, an official fan-club leader announces each number and whether it is a straight danzón composition like **Aniversario**, a pop tune or a bolero like **Lágrimas Negras**, it is transformed into a lush dance hall feast. The influence of the golden age of big bands is clear, yet Felipe, who began life playing clarinet in his local brass band, avoids an overproduced Hollywood sound. Like salsa, this is Latin dance music, but it is more subtle and less energetic – and the libido, always present on a Latin dance floor, is held just at arms length.

In the mid-1990s film *Danzón*, telephone operator María Rojo leaves her job on the Mexico City exchange in a quest to find her danzón partner. The film's success reflected the genre's continued grip on the popular imagination (danzón even became temporarily fashionable among the Mexico City elite). The public which follows Felipe Urbán around the dance halls six nights a week – policemen, secretaries, telephone operators – always have danced and always will dance danzón.

Mary Farquharson

Further listening: Acerina y su Danzonera's **Danzones** (Orfeon) showcases the orchestra of the late Acerina. **Centenario del Danzón** (Orfeon) is a 30-track double-CD compilation of the best-known danzones.

81

Cuco Valoy

Salsa con Coco

Kubaney, 1991

Cuco Valoy (vocals), Henry García (vocals), Raulín (vocals), Ramón Orlando (piano), Marcos Valoy (trombone), and others.

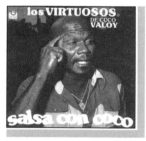

For an individual musician to defiantly call himself "El Brujo" (The Wizard) on his album sleeves and in his publicity takes *cojones*. But between the mid 1970s and mid 1980s, Cuco Valoy did just that, while leading a thir-teen-piece band he variously called La Tribu (The Tribe), Los Virtuosos (The Virtuosos) and La Nueva Tribu (The New Tribe).

Valoy's cultivated eccentricity – a strikingly shaved head while all around wore Afros – was based on an early understanding that his image would have to be rooted in his own personality, with-out playing down his race. The overriding impression he gave was of dignity and sobriety of purpose. He took his work, not least the organizational aspects, extremely seriously. As for the creative side, he was the introvert who needed a mask to be able to perform; he became the witch doctor.

Valoy's career had begun some time in the 1950s (he was always coy about his age and origins) with the duo, Los Ahijados (The Godchildren), formed with his brother Martín. This was unashamedly based on the Cuban fraternal duo, Los Compadres, and is a firm statement of intent – Cuco's abiding love of Cuban music, the son, would find equal expression with the traditions of his own Dominican culture, in the shape of merengue. Their guitar-accompanied duets were the first examples of the charac-teristically catarrhal vocals that would illuminate the sensual, sentimental, sassy songs that have since made him a star.

During his most productive era, with Los Virtuosos, an astonishingly high standard of song writing was matched by extraordinary live shows. Much of this was due to the writing and arranging of the band's pianist, Ramón Orlando – Cuco's son. With his brother Martín now on bass and another son, Marcos, on trombone, there were no problems of compatibility at the core of the organization. Add a second lead singer of the distinction of Henry García, impeccable percussion and a heartbreakingly sweet, sweet horn section, and the result was mesmerically compelling. Small wonder that he was universally accepted as "El Brujo".

Salsa Con Coco was released on vinyl in 1978, and is one of several titles re-released on CD by Kubaney (confusingly it also features songs from various other albums). It contains a slew of typically feisty Valoy tracks, including a version of **Guantanamera** that is almost a showcase of the band's reverence for their Cuban cousins' tradition. The song's broad social themes, with Valoy's own near-mystical musings added in, are projected with searing sincerity by Cuco at his rawest. A gentle, Cuban son montuno arrangement affords the lyrics a vehicle that remarkably transcends the banally familiar tune and chorus.

But the single tune which makes this CD essential is **Juliana**, the autobiographical tale of a piteous lad back home in Santo Domingo, writing to his love in New York, who left him months ago – with so many promises – for a new life on a three-day transit visa. "I'm not the first man to be bamboozled by a woman; my mother did warn me, but I was just an innocent. Juliana, *qué mala eres*" (Juliana, you're so bad). Such bittersweet recrimination tied to such a great melody, brilliantly arranged to reflect still palpable anger and regret – this is the quintessence of Cuco's sophisticated island swing, from his peak period.

Tommy Garcia

Further listening: 20 Éxitos de Los Ahijados (Kubaney) is the stripped-down sound of rural Cuba as interpreted by Cuco and Martín. **15 to Aniversario** (TTH), by Jossie Esteban y La Patrulla 15, is strictly merengue.

82

Los Van Van

Llegó... Van Van (Van Van Is Here)

Havana Caliente/Atlantic, 1999

Juan Formell (bass, leader, composer), César Pupi Pedroso (piano), Samuel Formell (drums, timbales), Pedrito Calvo, Mario Rivera, Roberto Hernández (vocals), Hugo Morejón (trombone, keyboards), and others.

Los Van Van are one of the most popular and musically astute orchestras in Cuba. **Llegó... Van Van**, which won a long overdue Grammy in 2000, is full of catchy melodies, with witty lyrics capturing contemporary Cuban concerns. Its themes are rooted in everyday life, personal relationships, and the potent Afro-Cuban santería religion.

Van Van have lasted more than thirty years at the top, with no sign of their dance-driven music losing its capacity to stay at the cutting edge. They produce several hits a year, from dance numbers like "El Buey Cansao" to the superb "La Habana No Aguanta Más" (Havana Can Take No More), about overcrowding in the capital. The band is led by bassist and innovator, Juan Formell, and it is his compulsion that keeps their music moving into new areas. Van Van's lyrics provide a history of the times, with many songs mapping key developments in Cuban life.

Formell founded Los Van Van in 1969, transforming the French-influenced charanga format with violins and flute by adding electric bass, synthesizers and a full drum kit. Together with his founding group of fifteen top calibre musicians, he created songo, a modernized version of son with a feel for developments in international salsa, jazz and rock, but still rooted in the percussive aesthetics of Nigerian Yoruba culture, with changing melodic timbres and unexpected harmonies.

Van Van's magic team included composer-pianist César "El Pupi" Pedroso, responsible along with Formell for many of Van Van's hits over the years, flautist José Luis Cortés, who later founded NG La Banda, and larger-than-life singer Pedro "Pedrito" Calvi, with his seductively, rich voice and outrageous dancing. In 1982 Formell added trombones. New members over the years have helped maintain the group's energy and youthful image, while their charismatic front line – Calvi, Mayito Rivera (Cuba's first dreadlocked singer) and Roberto Hernández Guayacán – makes them one of the greatest live bands.

In **Permiso Que Llegó Van Van**, the Afro-Cuban *orishas* (deities) praise Van Van's thirty years. The crisp drumming which opens the song heralds a track in which dense, layered arrangements are constructed from swathes of brass and synthesized riffs, underpinned by complex percussion. The santería theme reappears in **Appapas Del Calabar,** which celebrates the secret languages of the all-male Abakua cult.

A whole set of songs interlaced through the disc deal with the complications of relationships. The tremendous hit **Temba, Tumba, Timba** is a hilarious story of partner-swapping, filled with teasing puns and double-meanings referring to the music scene. The same frisky word-play is evident in the suggestive **El Negro Está Cocinando** (The Black One is Cooking): divorcee El Negro is relaxing by cooking Sunday lunch, and several female neighbours pop in to help with the different courses... **Mi Chocolate** is a lover's lament for his girl who has married an Italian – a consequence of tourism. It's a theme taken up again in the final, serenading melody of **Havana City**, which fuses Cubans' own passion for their city with concern for the future.

Jan Fairley

Further listening: in 1967 Formell radically renovated the son-changui of Elio Revé's Orquesta, a top outfit that can be heard on **La Explosión del Momento** (Real World). Orquesta Ritmo Oriental are one of Cuba's most beloved charanga típica bands; try **El Ritmo Oriental Te Está Llamando!** (Globestyle).

83

Adriana Varela

Cuando el Río Suena

Nueva Dirección de la Cultura, 1999

Adriana Varela (vocals), Jaime Roos (vocals, guitar, bass), Néstor Marconi, Toto D'Amario, José Malvares, Walter Castro, Leopoldo Federico, Miguel Trillo (bandoneón), Hugo Fattoruso, Gustavo Montemurro (accordion), Montevideo Philharmonic Orchestra, Los Mareados, Los Amantes de la Boca, and others.

Adriana Varela has been redefining and rejuvenating the tango scene with her deep, throaty voice and off-the-cuff eroticism for over a decade now, becoming Buenos Aires' most formidable contemporary female vocalist. Adopted in the late 1990s by the veteran maestros of tango song, Enrique Cadícamo and Roberto "Polaco" Goyeneche, her innate passion and sensual force was nurtured in an environment that allowed her to be both utterly contemporary and part of the evolving tradition of tango canción (tango song).

A young woman who had dared to be wholly woman in an often unremittingly macho scene might have been expected to stray beyond the bounds of tango, and **Cuando el Río Suena** (When the River Sings) is a major step. Exploring the folk tradition of the River Plate, with roots in both Buenos Aires and Montevideo, this multi-genre album sees Varela guiding herself into the more upbeat realms of the Afro-Uruguayan candombé style and the carnivalesque sound of the murga. Varela's strident voice is balanced perfectly with joyously freestyle choral arrangements, and backed by both contemporary rock instruments and traditional percussion (like the bombos and platillos – assorted drums and cymbals), the whole ensemble in the expert hands of

Uruguay's premier folk hero and multi-instrumentalist, Jaime Roos.

It is often said that Buenos Aires (unlike Montevideo) has its back to the river, hence the sophisticated, utterly urban and inward-looking spirit of tango. But in every Buenos Aires *barrio* (neighbourhood), murga bands still practice every Sunday, adults and kids gathering on the plazas to perform a strange, slightly aggressive but attractive strutting dance, to the chaotic clashing of bass and snare drums, cymbals and screeching whistles. The two murgas (**Aquello** and **Don Carlos**) which open *Cuando el Río Suena* contrast the riotous thumping of Argentine built on ensemble drumming – like Brazil's Carnival *blocos* – with the more celebratory chanting which takes place across the water. "Don Carlos" is a stunning example of delicious male choral voices softening Varela's soaring tones.

The two candombés, **Milongón del Guruyú** and **Ayer Te Vi**, show Varela breaking another cultural taboo, as Argentina has almost no remnants of its black slave population – they were wiped out by disease and wars – and this is easily the most African rhythm of southern South America. Both murga and candombé influenced tango dancing in the late nineteenth century – a detail often overlooked in white ballroom salons. The Roos-Varela duet **Pa'l Abrojal** is a tropical chamarra (a northeast Argentinian folk rhythm), gleefully alive with rural motifs and high-spirited onomatopoeias. Of course, Adriana Varela couldn't do an album without any tango and the range of styles contained here – from the trio style of the 1920s, through orchestral tango, to post-Astor Piazzolla fusion – is making the point that tango, in all its forms, is an integral part of the regional sound.

Chris Moss

Further listening: Varela sings straightahead tango on **Maquillaje** (Melopea Discos), with Lito Nebbia and friends; the album also incorporates tracks from the acclaimed cassette, *Tangos*, which juxtaposes classics with original, modern tango-like songs. **Amigos** (Melopea Discos) contains duet-tributes with Varela's mentor, Roberto Goyeneche, and shows off her range in ballads with Nebbia and others.

84

Chavela Vargas

30 Éxitos Acompañada Por Antonio Bribiesca

Orfeon, 1995.

Chavela Vargas (vocals), Antonio Bribiesca (guitar).

Chavela Vargas's journey to redis-covered fame and fortune, when over seventy years old, predated the Buena Vista Social Club phe-nomenon and was, in many ways, even more dramatic. Vargas began singing in bars and nightclubs during the Golden Age of Mexican music in the 1940s and 50s. Her repertoire, in a style known as ranchera, included songs by José Alfredo Jiménez and the more effete but equally bohemian Agustín Lara, a prolific and brilliant composer of boleros and songs that, like Jiménez's classics, still have plenty of life in them today.

Many other talented artists had a similar repertoire, but Vargas always stood out because of the emotional power of her singing. She didn't need trumpets or violins to drive home her message of love, loss and betrayal – indeed, the Mexican ranchera reper-toire only works when sung from the soul. Chavela still has a great, gritty voice but it is the experience of life, the abandon, the guts that she puts into this music, that grab hold and won't let go. In her heyday, Vargas also gained attention when she announced her homosexuality – at a time when such a declara-tion was hardly common. Her shows were dramatic affairs; look-ing back, she remembers nights when someone in the audience would shout "Chavela, put out that light!" – she would take a pistol from under her poncho and shoot the light bulb.

Drink eventually forced her to stop singing, and like so many other retired stars, she was assumed to be dead. When two leading cabaret artists and promoters, Jesusa Rodríguez and Liliana Felipe, discovered her living quietly in a village outside Mexico City, they invited her to give a few shows in their club, El Hábito. The result was phenomenal: crowds grew to overflow the club so she moved into bigger theatres and on to the major arts festivals, and even to the Olympia Theatre in Paris. By then she was the toast of Europe – Spanish film director Pedro Almodóvar joked that he wanted to marry her. Nowadays, like the Buena Vista veterans in Cuba, she only returns home to rest and prepare for the next presentation or prize in Madrid or Paris or Buenos Aires. But at the age of 81, she plans to retire from music with one last concert in Mexico, where her career began.

Vargas's recent recordings are beautifully produced, but her voice isn't the same second-time round and hence the best collections are the re-releases from her early days. Of these, the best without doubt is this double CD, on which Chavela is accompanied by the legendary guitarist Antonio Bribiesca, whose technical mastery and spirit enables him to get straight to the heart of the music. The album includes thirty songs, many of them anthems in Mexico today, including **Volver, Volver** – a love song which every Mexican and most Latin Americans know by heart – **Macorina**, **Arrieros Somos**, **Se Me Hizo Fácil**, and **Cruz de Olvido** – the last a popular lament about bearing the "Cross of Being Forgotten", replete with very Mexican references to Catholicism, cantinas, tequila and pistol shots.

Ranchera songs are more commonly performed by a melodramatic singer backed by weeping violins and the triumphant trumpets of a great mariachi band. On this superb disc, the same songs are stripped naked by Antonio Bribiesca's exquisite guitar, while Chavela's tequila-stained voice speaks a universal language.

Mary Farquharson

Further listening: the first of the great divas, Lucha Reyes, captures the spirit of ranchera music at its peak on **15 Éxitos** (BMG). Astrid Hadad shows off her tremendous ranchera voice on **Ay** (Continental), combining humour with melodrama but never losing respect for the music.

85

Wilfrido Vargas

Serie 2000

BMG, 2000

Wilfrido Vargas (vocals, trumpet, arrangements); no other musicians credited.

If it was Johnny Ventura who first dragged the merengue gyrating and chanting into the late twentieth century, it was Wilfrido Vargas who completed the process, embracing synthesizers, thumping bass patterns, shell suits, gold chains and a pan-Latin wheeler-dealer management ethos linking Santo Domingo with Miami and New York. Yet the Dominican Republic's national rhythm still retained a powerful tang of old country merengue, of rednecks dancing pegaíto with minimal movement, the body clenched Hispanically in the attitude described locally as "chewing gum in the ass".

Wilfrido Vargas was born in 1949 in Altamira, near the northern coastal town of Puerto Plato, to an accordionist father and flautist mother who monitored their son's early musical adventures closely. These included tuition in the municipal Academy of Music, where he earned the right to use one of the few trumpets. This feat was followed by a precocious appointment as first trumpet of the Altamira Municipal Band at the age of eleven – before the family moved to the capital Santo Domingo, where Vargas supported himself as a postman, until he was sacked.

In 1972, his assiduous gigging led him to a nightclub named the Casbah, where he put together a five-piece house band, named, in deference to the place's Arab theme, Los Beduinos. Within a year they had expanded into a full-size merengue outfit, and a vehicle for Vargas's energetic experimentations. He added tthe bubbling guitar and hissing hi-hats of Haitian "mini-jazz" bands, plus the heavy bouncing bass and drum sound of Trinidadian soca and Martiniquan zouk. He drove the percussion section further along the conga-boosted path pioneered by Johnny Ventura, tightened the rhythmic intensity of the squawking saxophone section, and added his trademark silver trumpet.

In 1978, the album, *Punto y Aparte!*, featuring the hit song **El Barbarazo**, confirmed Vargas as merengue's top creative force, a status he confirmed by taking on a series of successful protégés. The Santo Domingo press was inspired to speak of the "Wilfridization" of merengue. In the case of Las Chicas del Can, a gaudily glamorous girl band resembling fourteen Creole Barbara Windsors, allegations circulated that he had created all their music himself. The Chicas rejected such claims as macho condescension.

Machismo, of course, exudes freely from Vargas's productions, as do the boisterously politically incorrect attitudes without which popular merengue would be neither popular nor merengue. Witness the great hits, **Abusadora**, which lambasts a no-good temptress, or **El Africano**, whose nubile ingenue heroine is harassed by an earthy black male – a big salsa hit in the 1980s. There is something of the conveyor belt about his dance floor productions, particularly on the songs with associated dance steps, such as **Baile Del Perrito** (Little Dog Dance) and **El Mono** (The Monkey) – neither of which are entirely dignified.

Vargas's prodigious output has attracted criticism. His merenguified salsa numbers and ballads – **Volveré** is a prime example – were even dubbed *fusilamientos*, or musical executions by firing squad. What nobody can gainsay is his single-minded genius for exciting arrangements, a talent that bursts out of those devastating Vargas brass interludes. These are little jewels of rhythm – all so similar, yes, but all so unendingly, irresistibly effective.

Philip Sweeney

Further listening: Sergio Vargas – Wilfrido's protégé, but no relation – adds roots touches to his mellifluous productions on **Este Es Mi País** (Sony). Top 1990s Santo Domingo band, Pochy and the Cocoband demonstrate their energy and precision on the greatest hits album, **Grandes Éxitos** (Kubaney).

86

Los Vasallos del Sol

Tibio Calor

Bigott, 1999

Jesús Rondón (leader), Eloísa Pérez, Sobeida Martínez, Betsaida Machado, Isabel Loero, Ángel Palacios, Antonio Clemente, César Gómez (vocals); Carlos Martínez (cuatro), Juan Carlos Rico, Jesús Raúl Paiva, Juan José Salazar (percussion).

The slave trade touched virtually every corner of the Americas but nowhere was its impact more profound than on the Caribbean and Atlantic coasts. Today, along Venezuela's pristine Caribbean shore, village after village looks and sounds remarkably African. From the huge five-foot long wooden mina drums of Curiepe to the bamboo percussion quitiplas of Barlovento, the music of this region is truly African.

Los Vasallos del Sol (Servants of the Sun) were founded in 1990, a natural offshoot of the Talleres de Cultura Popular de Fundación Bigott, a cultural centre located in the middle of Caracas. It is Venezuela's largest private arts institute, and runs classes, workshops and performances dedicated to traditional art, theatre, music and dance. The band's name is derived from the influence in the region of solar festivals – *parranda* at Christmas and *sangeo* during the San Juan festival, at June's summer solstice.

The first Vasallo was Jesús Rondón, who now acts as the group's musical director. Since its inception, the group has been the leading exponent of Afro-Venezuelan folk music. The repertoire includes sangeo (from a West African word, *sanga*, which means "to dance while walking slowly"), which is similar to Colombian cumbia, and parranda, or Afro-Venezuelan Christmas carols. They also play calipso, a style brought over from Trinidad during the nineteenth-century gold rush. While these styles of music can be heard in villages across Venezuela, Los Vasallos were the first group to produce professional recordings. They were also the first to promote their work internationally – with a full entourage of 26 musicians and dancers. They are, perhaps, Venezuela's answer to the better-known Afro-Cuban rumba band, Los Muñequitos de Matanzas.

Tibio Calor (Tepid Heat) is the group's greatest recording achievement. The CD opens with **Si Yo Fuera**, a Venezuelan Christmas parranda. Under Jesús Rondón's masterful direction, Vasallos del Sol's interpretation includes a massive percussive foundation, guitars, local cuatro guitars, and an entire chorus of female vocalists. It's an incredibly moving recording, not least for the presence of the often-overlooked Venezuelan calipso. Sung in Spanglish, and based on an Andalucian chord structure, there are several calipso tracks featured on this disc, including **Tanty Ernestine**, on which Angel Palacios's evocative and dynamic voice leads an acoustic guitar-driven sound.

But the group is best known for its interpretations of Afro-Venezuelan drum and vocal styles, which, in the live shows, are set to elaborate choreography. With songs such as **Julio Moreno**, a song about a man who sells bread, and the work song, **Canto de Lavanderas** (Song Of the Washerwomen), they produce a sound reminiscent of a cross between Sweet Honey and the South African vocal group, Ladysmith Black Mambazo. Add to that a percussion layer almost as massive as Dudu N'Diaye Rose's forty-drum Senegalese orchestra. The only drawback to this CD is that you can't see Los Vasallos's mesmerizing dance accompaniment of twelve to fourteen dancers, mixing athleticism, acrobatics, flirtatiousness and dazzling choreography.

Dan Rosenberg

Further listening: Un Solo Pueblo's **20 Años** (Sonografica, Venezuela) is a career-spanning greatest hits collection of the pop-crossover equivalent to Los Vasallos del Sol. Guaco's **Como Era y Como Es** (Latin World) is a great example of how the Venezuelan group integrates Venezuelan rhythms such as the gaita and joropo, with elements of rock'n'roll, funk, jazz and salsa.

87

Belô Velloso

Belô Velloso

Velas, 1996

Belô Velloso (vocals), João Cantiber (guitar), Dodô Ferreira (bass), Firmino (percussion), Ricardo Rente (sax), Sacha Amback (keyboards), Maria Bethânia, Caetano Veloso (guest vocals).

Two of the most promising younger women singers to emerge in Brazil during the 1990s both have illustrious pedigrees. Bebel Gilberto is the daughter of João Gilberto, one of the founders of bossa nova. And Belô Velloso is the niece of both Maria Bethânia, one of the most accomplished and respected singers of her generation, and Caetano Veloso, arguably Brazilian music's leading figure. The family resemblance is physically striking. Veloso and Bethânia turn up on different tracks of this excellent debut album, lending more than just moral support, but Belô didn't need anyone's help to carve out her own reputation as one of the most promising new stars of MPB (*música popular brasileira*).

After four albums of uniformly excellent quality, Belô has a substantial body of work. This, her debut album, has all the freshness of a self-confident new talent exploding onto the scene, and not a single weak track. It also has her two biggest hits to date: the boppy, up-tempo **Só Penso Nela** and the dreamy, sensuous **Toda Sexta Feira**, which was one of the most popular radio songs of the decade. Still in her twenties, Belô looks set to follow the trail blazed by Marisa Monte to international stardom. Belô's voice, as one would expect of a Velloso, is extraordinarily good, with perfect pitch and control and a rather jazzy style. She experiments with different styles and arrangements, and has no regular backing band, preferring to work with top studio musicians. Indeed, her music lends itself better to the studio and she hasn't yet mastered the art of live performance.

Belô's talent is immediately obvious from the first tracks, a jazzy, off-centre reworking of an old Caetano song, **Mamãe Coragem**, followed by a good-humoured duet with Aunt Bethânia in **Brincando**, where you can almost hear Maria Bethânia's proud smile through her singing. Caetano turns up a couple of tracks later, duetting on **Amante Amado**. This was a lively dance number when played by its composer, Jorge Ben Jor, but here it is slowed down and the rhythm is broken up. It is transformed into a tender love song.

But it is the final two tracks that best showcase Belô's voice. "Só Penso Nela", the most uptempo song on the album, is a sunny, gorgeously sung love song and a fine prelude to the outstanding "Toda Sexta Feira", a dreamy, relaxed gem so reminiscent of beaches and lazing in the sun that you can practically feel the sand between your toes. Belô's voice, stretching the phrases, tailing off and coming on again with perfect timing, is as haunting as the words: Every Friday/all clothes white/all skin black/all sky magenta/every Friday/everyone Bahian together…

There is something very Bahian about Belô Velloso. Bahia, her native state, is famous for its beaches, Afro-Brazilian culture, and the frenetic dance music of its Carnival, but it also has a languid, quiet and sensual side – a tradition often reflected musically in the work of Caetano and Maria Bethânia. It is this aspect of Bahia that Belô embodies in this album; it is quiet, reflective, intimate music – mostly love songs – and the overall effect is extraordinarily sexy. It is no accident the inside cover photo is a bed with rumpled sheets. Remarkably, at twenty-five Belô proves herself as much essence of Bahia as her aunt and uncle.

David Cleary

Further listening: more uptempo than Belô's first release is her excellent Um **Segundo** (Velas). Tom Zé's **Brazil Classics 5: Return Of** (Luaka Bop), is an idiosyncratic and often bizarre compilation of Brazilian songs.

88

Caetano Veloso

Estrangeiro

Island, 1990

Caetano Veloso (guitar, vocals, lyrics), Arto Lindsay (guitar, vocals), Peter Sherer (keyboards), Nana Vasconcelos (percussion, vocals), Bill Frisell, Marc Ribot, Toni Costa (guitar), Tavinho Fialho (bass), Tony Lewis, Cesinha (drums), Carlinhos Brown (percussion).

Brazilian superstar Caetano Veloso is a renaissance man. A singer-songwriter and a prime mover in post-1960s Brazilian popular music (MPB), he is also a respected poet, painter and, latterly, video director. In the 35 years since he recorded "Alegria, Alegria", he has sold over six million records worldwide. Among his 34 albums – almost one a year, to date – **Estrangeiro** (The Foreigner) is the classic.

Caetano wrote his first songs – love ballads and protest songs with social and political messages – when he was studying philosophy in Salvador de Bahia, in northeast Brazil, in the mid 1960s. He was part of a clique of talented young idealists, including Gilberto Gil, Gal Costa and his sister Maria Bethânia, who shared a passion for new English and US pop, particularly The Beatles, though they were also fiercely proud of their Bahian musical traditions. They called themselves the *tropicalistas*. Their radical songs targeted Brazil's military dictatorship and Veloso and Gil were accused of anti-nationalism for adopting "foreign music" and electric guitars – and for their "dangerous" lyrics. They were arrested in 1971 and offered prison or exile; they chose London. Returning in 1972 to a hero's (or a pop star's) welcome, they resumed their careers at the highest level.

Although tropicália broke with many musical traditions, Caetano was influenced by bossa nova in the delicate languor of his voice. But for this late-1980s album, he invited two New York producers from the avant-garde: white-noise electric guitarist Arto Lindsay and Swiss keyboard player Peter Sherer (from the Ambitious Lovers). Veloso balanced the US contingent with two formidable percussionists, Nana Vasconcelos and the young Bahian, Carlinhos Brown. In spite of their reputations for loud, expressionistic music, and sonic experiments with guitars, the New Yorkers' moody backdrops lent extra dimension and mood to the mix, without overwhelming the Brazilian sound.

The *tropicalistas* developed an early passion for reggae that has characterized their songs ever since. **Outro Retrato** has a funky bass lead and twiddly guitars, and culminates in a Brazilian-Jamaican jam. **Meia Lua Inteira** is a jumpy samba-reggae delight, darting and jerking like a *capoeira* dancer. The lyrics of the title track, **O Estrangeiro**, mix the themes of love and politics while the music moves to a choppy reggae-samba beat with a subtle industrial guitar-chaos backing. Like the sharper **Os Outros Romanticos**, it is a mini-musical epic. The guitarists have a freer reign, and their electronic effects blend with brisk samba-school percussion to create an appropriate edginess.

Bossa nova drifts all through the album, most pleasingly on the seductive **Branquinha**, a poem about idealized love. Caetano and Arto sing in English, the New Yorker's falsetto cutting across softly angular bossa rhythms, while scraping electric guitar effects maintain love's tensions. The album's catchiest song, **Genipapo Absoluto**, is another seductive love song peppered with the melancholy that accompanies great love (described in that very Brazilian concept, *saudade*). A beautiful ending to the album, its melody hangs in the air long after the abrupt ending.

Sue Steward

Further listening: Circulado Vivo (Polygram, Brazil) is a brilliant live set of old and new songs from 1993. Moreno Veloso's beautiful debut, **Music Typewriter** (Hannibal, 2001), reveals the uncannily similar voice of Veloso Junior as he takes MPB into a new age.

89

Johnny Ventura

20th Anniversary

Sony Discos, 1999

No musicians credited.

Juan de Dios Ventura Soriano, aka Johnny Ventura, moved the merengue into the modern era, and in the process became a Latin star to rival the founding salsa artists. Originally a folk genre mixing European salon dance with African percussion, the merengue is the traditional rhythm of the Dominican Republic, built on a galloping 2/4 rhythm interspersed with cascading instrumental riffs known as *jaleos*. During the thirty-year rule of the spectacularly sanguinary dictator Trujillo, which ended with his assassination in 1961, the merengue was promoted as the country's National Music.

Johnny Ventura was born in 1940 in the capital, Santo Domingo, and began singing in the late 1950s. Spotted at an amateur concert by the President's brother, Petán Trujillo, who owned the radio station La Voz Dominicana, Ventura was given a grant to study music, and by the end of the decade was finding success with his good looks and rich, vital voice. In 1959, he made his first LP and adopted his new stage name for pressing reasons entirely unrelated to showbusiness: one Captain Juan de Dios Ventura Simó, an anti-Trujillo activist totally unrelated to Ventura, was captured and shot. Even a chance similarity of name could lead to trouble in Trujillo's Dominican Republic.

By 1963, Ventura was singing with the leading Super Orquesta San José, but post-Trujillo political relaxation and the advent of rock inspired him to create a smaller, more modern group.

Supported by a nightclub entrepreneur, Ventura formed his Combo Show, a thirteen-member group with a reduced saxophone section but boosted percussion. With Ventura handling arrangements, the Combo Show developed a faster, harder, more richly syncopated style of merengue. Looking to the black American soul revues, he dressed the musicians in ritzy modern costumes and choreographed exciting synchronized dance routines. It was a huge success, making Ventura a television star at home and a Dominican hero abroad, as Latin communities in New York, Miami, Caracas and Bogotá all fell for the tall, dark Santo Domingo Elvis. By the 1990s, Ventura was also a substantial political figure at home, eventually becoming Vice-Mayor of Santo Domingo.

Over four decades, Ventura has built a major repertoire, including salsa, boleros and the occasional ballad, but it's mainly merengues that he plays, many self-penned. Often, as in **El Muerto Parrandero**, **Seremos Tres**, or **La Cirugía**, they feature typically Dominican baudy subject matter, with corpses getting up to party, doctors performing double entendre-laden operations on women, and housewifely hanky-panky with neighbours.

Ventura never neglects his roots: **Merenguero Hasta La Tambora** (A Merengue-Player Right to the Tambora – a reference to the horizontally-held double-headed tambora drum that sets the rumbling beat in a merengue group) is a composition by the great Joseíto Mateo, Ventura's predecessor, while 1990's rustic-accented **La Inseminación** harks back to the older, slower country merengues of the Cibao Valley with its lilting, synthesized accordion figure. And everything Ventura records has a savoury mixture of tight, hypnotic saxophone *jaleos*, judicious percussion, rich lead vocals trading against an exciting chorus – and sheer swing.

Philip Sweeney

Further listening: Merengue, Dominican music and Dominican Identity (Rounder) is a first-class collection of historical and modern, rural and urban merengues, and includes Joseíto Mateo, Ventura's model. **A Caballo** (J&N/Sony) is a homage to Ventura from merengue's recent bright star and Ventura's natural successor, Kinito Méndez.

90

Paulinho da Viola

Bebadosamba

BMG/RCA, 1996

Paulinho da Viola (vocals, cavaquinho), Jorge Filho (cavaquinho), Celsinho Silva, Cabelinho, Hercules, Wilson das Neves (percussion), Cristóvão Bastos (piano), Célsio Farias (guitar), Zé Nogueira (sax), Mário Séve (flute, sax), Dininho (bass).

There are two kinds of samba. There is the rough, rootsy street music of early samba greats like Cartola, from samba's golden age between the 1920s and 1950s, and there is the softer, lyrical and more musically complex style developed since. The undisputed master of the latter is Paulinho da Viola. Born – where else? – in Rio, in 1942, his musical inventiveness, soft singing voice and genius for lyrics have established him as the grand old man of samba, a bastion of integrity and loyalty to samba's roots in an age of glitzy commercialization.

Like all great *sambistas*, Paulinho da Viola is linked to a samba *escola*, one of the huge samba schools which parade through Rio as the highlight of the city's Carnival. Many of his sambas are written for his beloved Escola Portela but, in a protest against the domination of samba by commercial interests and a concern more for promoting tourism than for regarding Carnival's origins as street music, Paulinho left Portela in 1990 and founded a new *escola*, Quilombo. With Quilombo, he was dedicated to preserving Afro-Brazilian Carnival culture, and made a point of not competing in the official Carnival parades.

Paulinho's style of samba owes a great deal to choro, a slower, jazz- and tango-influenced style of samba that emerged in the 1930s. It extended the range of instruments used beyond the traditional percussion, guitar and cavaquinho (a miniature guitar with a sound like a picked banjo) to take in flute, sax, piano and violin. To this mix Paulinho adds a lyrical genius, an ability to put new twists on the eternal samba themes of love lost and found, and on samba's characteristic emotions of irony and nostalgia.

After releasing a string of outstanding samba and choro records from the 1960s through to the end of the 1980s, Paulinho stopped recording for seven years, depressed by what he saw as samba's betrayal of its roots with the increasing obsession with Carnival as tourist spectacle. In 1996, **Bebadosamba** (a pun, it translates as both "Drunk On Samba" and "Drink In Samba") marked a triumphant return to record. It is beautifully played and beautifully arranged classic, contemporary samba, and its quality shows up much current samba for the commercial dreck it is. The record alternates between slower, choro-influenced sambas (**Quando A Samba Chama, Alento, Novos Rumos**) and more upbeat, good-time dance numbers of the style known as samba-canção (**É Difícil Viver Assim, O Ideal É Competir**). Both are marked by Paulinho's lyrical genius.

The album also marks a mending of bridges with the Portela samba school. "O Ideal É Competir" is a straight hymn of praise to the *escola*, with backing vocals and marvellous percussion from Portela's rhythm section. The highlights are probably the final two tracks, **Mar Grande**, a stunning slow samba with virtuoso cavaquinho accompaniment by Jorge Filho, and the title track, where Paulinho ends in typical style by invoking a long list of samba stars, beginning with Cartola. The greatest living *sambista* paying tribute to the greatest *sambista* in history, while taking samba into its second century.

David Cleary

Further listening: Cantando (RCA/Victor) features vintage sambas from Paulinho's most productive period. **Chorando** (RCA/Victor) is a gem, an entire album of intimate, quiet and relaxing choro. **Eu Canto Samba** (RCA/Victor), "I Sing Samba", is the defiant title of Paulinho's last record before he withdrew in disgust from the samba scene.

91

Carlos Vives

Clásicos de la Provincia

Virgin, 2000

Carlos Vives (guitar, vocals), Egidio Cuadrado (accordion, vocals), Heberth
Cuadrado (box drum, vocals), Eder Polo (guacharaca), Ernesto "Teto" Ocampo,
Anibal Rivera (guitar), Antonio Arnedo (bagpipe, sax), Bernardo Ossa (keyboards,
percussion), Michael Egizi (piano), Luis Angel Pastor (bass), and others.

Carlos Vives sprung a surprise in
1993 when, with his band La
Provincia, he regenerated the
hot, sweet accordion-led dance
music of Colombia known as vallenato by infusing it with pop,
rock and a little bit more. He will
be a pivotal figure for a new generation that has embraced the
innovations of older contemporaries like Juan Luis Guerra, who
reinvented Dominican bachata and merengue, and Rubén
Blades, who transformed the conventions of salsa.

Vallenato music takes its name from Valledupar, on Colombia's
Atlantic coat. It is fast, driving music, characterized by the individual musical quirks of local composers who have subtly
absorbed African percussion timbres and indigenous Indian
influences. The attractive and charismatic Vives was initially a
star of Colombian tele-soap, playing a leading vallenato composer called Rafael Escolona. His songs became well-loved tunes,
and the role ultimately led to this groundbreaking album,
Clásicos de la Provincia (Classics by La Provincia/Provincial
Classics), which pays homage to the key composers of the genre.

The magic of Vives derives from the way he captures the
defining individual styles of veteran vallenato composers, aided
by the stunning accordionist Egidio Cuadrado, without over-

sentimentalizing. The tremendous impact of this disc had as much to do with its celebration of tradition as its subversion. As he cries at the end of the extremely sexist **La Celosa** (The Jealous One), "I know a song even worse than that one!"

The album draws heavily on the rapport and shared attitude of a group of consummate young musicians who play with almost teasing pleasure and a lot of playful passion. The album opens with the roots-rock harmonies of **La Gota Fría**, accented by the mellifluous sound of Indian flutes. An accordion jumps in with a typically irresistible melody line then Vives's voice enters, gently and lyrically, partnered by a light, female-dominated chorus. While the general mood of the disc is true to vallenato's jaunty attitude, the precise way in which the band deftly introduces touches of musical detail has an almost tender feel.

Vallenato music is gorgeous to dance to. Its structures lean heavily on Colombian cumbia, built on embracing folk couple-dance moves. By adding driving bass-lines, dynamic drumming and an infectious guitar to the traditional accordion, pipes and box drums, Vives's band had accentuated the rhymic layers of vallenato's usual 6/8 swing without losing its gently shifting 1-2 pulse, as with the funky **La Tijera**.

The hauntingly romantic introduction by soprano sax on Alejo Durán's **Altos De Rosario** captures the mournful side of the genre, an aspect also vividly expressed in **Alicia Adorada**, a romantic favourite about an ideal love who dies young. Vives enabled young Colombians to embrace the rural sounds of their elders, and the impact of his music in urban Bogotá somewhat humanized the reputation of the notorious city. The ricocheting rhythms and anecdotal lyrics of **La Hamaca Grande** (The Big Hammock) sum up the genre: "a beautiful serenade played on the accordion from the land of the hammock".

Jan Fairley

Further listening: Putumayo Presents Colombia (Putumayo) offers a keen selection of contemporary Colombian sounds. **Bloque, Bloque** (Luaka Bop) sees La Provincia's Ivan Benavides lead a new wave band taking a rock approach to a folk-inspired collection of songs.

92

Atahualpa Yupanqui

Lo Mejor de Atahualpa Yupanqui

BMG Ariola, South America/Spain

Atahualpa Yupanqui (guitar, vocals).

Atahualpa Yupanqui was hugely influential all over Latin America since the 1950s for his songs, solo guitar compositions and virtuoso guitar technique. Garlanded with awards right up to his death in 1992, he travelled the world, even meeting Picasso and Edith Piaf, who befriended him when he first came to Paris in 1948.

Hector Roberto Chavero Uramburu was born in 1908 and spent his youth as an itinerant musician, riding a horse across the pampas, learning from nomadic *gaucho* cowboys and traditional musicians in out-of-the-way places. He arrived from Tucumán to Buenos Aires when he was eighteen and changed his name around the same time, in homage to his Amerindian ancestors. With songs like **Camino del Indio** (Path of the Indian), written when he was only twenty, he quickly became a musical legend, renowned for placing the Indian experience at the centre of his musical world.

Yupanqui's approximately 1500 works, of which sixteen appear here, rank alongside those of his Chilean contemporary, Violeta Parra. They potently inspired the next generation of musicians, those involved in the 1960s and 70s struggles for social and political reform – usually referred to as the nueva canción (New Song) movement. Like so many, Yupanqui saw his music banned, and he was imprisoned several times in the 1940s, when he opposed his country's military government. "They'll have to break my guitar to stop me singing," he said. **Guitarra**

Dímelo Tú anticipates nueva canción as he communes with his guitar, searching for a ray of light. **Trabajo, Quiero Trabajo** (Work, I Want Work) is a cry against a familiar injustice.

The singer's deep, at times almost gruff voice introduces twelve of these pieces. He employed traditional Argentine musical styles – vidala, milonga, baguala, zamba, chacarera, malambo – to capture, with great simplicity, the almost devastating sense of solitude and space of the under-populated interior. Such themes are explored in **Le Tengo Rabia Al Silencio** (I Am Angry at the Silence), **El Promesante** (The Promise), about an endless journey, and the classic **Los Ejes De Mi Carreta** (The Axles of My Cart), which conjures the loneliness of a long journey with only the creaking of the wheels for company.

La Copla, a baguala (mountain song), distills the history of harsh Indian lives, while drawing attention to the fact that most Yupanqui lyrics follow the traditions of the old Spanish *copla* (couplet) form, with its eight-syllable rhyming lines. On his evocative **La Tarde** (The Evening), Yupanqui's reedy voice describes the countryside at twilight, as animals disappear and the guitar leaves trace notes in the air. The man-and-nature theme is echoed in **A La Noche La Hizo Dios** (God Made The Night), **El Aromo** (The Wild Tree), **El Alazán** (The Sorrel Horse) and the compelling **Paisaje Con Nieve** (Landscape with Snow), which describes a condor high in the sky.

In **El Poeta**, Yupanqui, a poet with charismatic, sculpted Indian features, advises living among the people and "singing of their struggle for a piece of bread". In **El Pampino** (The Indian), he describes a life caught between harsh sun and relentless work. His themes are ruminative, his texts simple yet hugely resonant, their mournfulness offset by the truths they capture and, at times, the almost sacred tone.

Jan Fairley

Further listening: Raúl Barboza (Night and Day, France), the King of chamamé, from northeast Argentina, plays accordion-rich rhythms with Indian influences. Guitarist Eduardo Falú plays Argentine rural dances with a classical edge on **Resolana: Songs from Argentina** (Nimbus).

93

Various Artists

Antología del Son de México

Discos Corasón, 1993

Various artists, including Juan Reynoso, Conjunto Poker de Ases, Los Hermanos Molina and Helidoro Copado.

Since it was first produced, as a six-LP box set in 1982 (it now squeezes onto three CDs), this "Anthology of Mexican son" has become an inspiration to Mexican musicians from Los Lobos to Café Tacuba, and from Ely Guerra to Los Folkloristas. It is acknowledged as the most important musical reference for Mexican son – the fiery, syncopated, string-band music that is played over much of Central Mexico. Mexican son is a kind of super-genre spanning a wide range of styles, from the percussive harps and guitars of son jarocho, and the soaring violins and falsetto voices of son huasteco, to the thumping rhythms of the big harps of Michoacan culture, and the sweet istmeno son, which is the most European-sounding style.

Part of what makes the collection so enjoyable is that is was recorded, selected and produced by three musical fanatics who simply travelled around central and southwest Mexico listening to bands in towns, villages and ranches, at parties and brothels and bars, recording whatever they found irresistible. Their tastes led them far from the bright lights and fanfare of the city recording studios to unknown musicians playing music they had inherited from their fathers and grandfathers.

The three CDs – available separately, as well as in the box set, which contains a comprehensive booklet – are divided by region, each of which has its own style of traditional country music. The norteño (Tex-Mex) style is not included, and neither is marimba music from the south. The first CD includes the spectacular sones de la Tierra Caliente ("Son from the Hot Lands" – the Rio Balsas region), which bring to light the genius of violinist Juan Reynoso. It also presents unknown mariachi bands that play sones de Jalisco as they sounded before the mariachis became commercialized in the 1950s. The CD also includes recordings of the spectacular big harps that play the sones calentanos from the Tepalcatepec basin (a scorchingly hot region in the fairly wild West) and the poetic son arribeño from the Sierra Gorda mountains, in central Mexico.

The second disc presents uncommercial versions of the sones jarochos from Veracruz. After mariachi music, this is the most widely known style of son beyond its home territory, and it has been revived by the younger, World Music generation, who have fused it with other styles. From the Pacific coast come sones and chilenas from Costa Chica, and, from a little further south, the Zapotecs' son istmeno – a sweet and very infectious string-band style which is sung in Zapotec Indian to a more gentle rhythm.

The third CD is dedicated entirely to son huasteco, a somewhat miraculous genre: how three musicians (a violin and two guitars and voices) can produce such complete and emotionally intense music is a mystery. **El San Lorenzo**, for instance, featuring the falsetto of Marcos Hernández and the improvised flights of the violin of Heliodoro Copado, is a hair-raising experience. The extreme passion of this music might not be to all tastes, but for those who like their traditional music undiluted by commercial fashion or international fusion experiments, this is where it's at.

Mary Farquharson

Further listening: Traditional harpist and singer La Negra Graciana exemplifies the son jarocho tradition on **Sones Jarochos** (Discos Corasón) Mono Blanco were in the vanguard of the son jarocho revival of the early 1980s; try **El Mundo Se Va A Acabar** (Urtext) **La Tortuga** (Discos Corasón) is an excellent collection of string-band son istmeno from Oaxaca.

94

Various Artists

Brazil Classics 2: O Samba

Luaka Bop, 1989

Clara Nunes, Zeca Pagodinho, Alcione, Ciro Moneiro, Beth Carvalho, Neguinho da Beija Flor, Chico da Silva, Almir Guineto, Agepê, Martinho da Vila and Paulinho da Viola.

These days, the record store bins seem to be bursting with throngs of new Brazilian compilations, a far cry from the mid 1980s, when David Byrne took a hiatus from Talking Heads and took off to South America in search of his other passion, Brazilian music. The series of albums resulting from these trips, *Brazil Classics*, redefined the music business by selling over half a million copies.

As the title suggests, the second volume is dedicated to Brazil's most infectious rhythm, a sound that is synonymous with Rio de Janeiro: samba. The style is a complex mix of influences, including Angolan semba (where it gets its name), European polka, Argentinian tango, African batuques, Afro-Brazilian lundo and Cuban habanera – among other styles. What we now know as samba was the result of the arrival of black Brazilians, primarily from Bahia, in the *favelas* (shanty towns) surrounding Rio, following the abolition of slavery in Brazil in 1888.

Brazil Classics 2: O Samba is a Who's Who of *sambista* legends, and it also demonstrates that there is much more to samba than the fast paced soundtrack to scantily clad carnival dancing. The album appropriately begins with two tracks from the legendary singer Clara Nunes, who died tragically in 1983 when her brain lost oxygen during a minor surgical operation on varicose veins. With her magical voice that brought together the children of three races, Nunes was known for both incredible passion and heartfelt tenderness. Here, on *O Samba*, are two gems that highlight her Afro-Brazilian roots: **A Deusa Dos Orixás** and **Ijexa: Filhos De Gandhí**, the latter a samba version of the anthem of Salvador de Bahia's famous percussion ensemble, Filhos de Gandhi.

Among the most touching songs are the mid-tempo samba ballads. The late Agepê's **Ela Não Gosta De Mim** is a passionate story of lost love set to the trademark *carioca* (Rio-based) sound of cavaquinho (a small banjo-like guitar), percussion and cuica (squeaky drum) – the cries of the latter mimicking Agepê's pain. Brazil's reigning king of samba, the crooner Martinho da Vila, contributes two standout tracks, including **Claustrofobia,** which spotlights his deep, smoky voice. Meanwhile, Neguinho da Beija Flor's **Oldeia De Okarimbe** captures the infectious non-stop energy of Rio's famous carnival samba schools, as hundreds of singers and drummers are synchronized by the power and precision of Beija Flor's athletic vocal power.

Another strength of the collection is how it shows off samba's diversity. Zeca Pagodinho's **S.P.C.** (Serviço de Proteção Ao Credito – Credit Bureau) is a humorous topical song about the perils of shopping with bad credit. On the political side, in **Olerê Camará**, Alcione asks the men playing *capoeira* (an Afro-Brazilian dance-cum-martial art) to "open up the circle", implying more than opening the circle of the game and suggesting opening up the male-dominated tradition to women. Taken as a whole, *O Samba* is one of those rare albums where you can put away your remote control and enjoy fifteen infectious gems, all of which deserve the distinction of being called "Brazilian Classics."

Dan Rosenberg

Further listening: The Best of Clara Nunes (World Pacific) is a magnificent collection of twenty samba classics from Nunes's tragically short career. **The Rough Guide to Samba** (World Music Network), another compilation, brings a whole new take on the samba greats.

95

Various Artists

Brazil Classics 3: Forró

Luaka Bop, 1991

Luiz Gonzaga, Dominguinhos, Anastácia, Jackson do Pandeiro, Genival Lacerda, João do Vale, Trio Nordestino, Pinto do Acordeon, Marinalva, Clemilda, Nando Cordel, Jorge de Altinho, Amelinha and Elba Ramalho.

"A palm-leaf roof, a dirt dance-floor, hundreds of eager towns-folk" – the notes to this wonderful compilation of music from northeastern Brazil describe a scene a world away from the familiar urban sounds of bossa nova and samba. Yet the jaunty rhythms and bittersweet, Portuguese-influenced melodies of forró take some beating.

Various stars of MPB (Brazilian Popular Music) have worked to take forró music into the mainstream but it took this compilation by the adventurous David Byrne, to reach international markets.

The musical "king" of the region was the composer-singer-accordionist Luiz Gonzaga (born in 1912), who became popular by bringing this regional music to the migrant workers living in Rio and São Paulo. His extensive output – he recorded about five hundred songs and released more than two hundred records – has been inspirational for musicians following in his footsteps, many of whom appear on this album. Gonzaga first forged the style known as baião in the 1940s, shaping it from folk dances, and later developed forró (a word evolved from parties thrown "for all" by British railway engineers) from a mixture of European, African and indigenous influences. These elements can be heard on Gonzaga's celebratory **Danado de Bom**

The disc kicks off with a late Gonzaga piece, **O Fole Roncou** a foot-tapping party groove played by a classic forró trio comprising robust accordion, tinkling triangle and rich zambumba bass drum; the gravely, nasal tones of the singer are typical. The same format reappears in Trio Nordestino's melancholy **Rejeição**, which features Gonzaga's accordion heir, Pinto do Acordeon. A sad song about rejection, a sweet answering chorus provides a foil to the muted anger of the vocals.

At the heart of the disc is Luiz Gonzaga's emotive **Asa Branca**, a massive Brazilian hit in the 1940s. It became the hymn of the northeast for its nostalgic melody and lyrics – it compares a migrant worker and a white dove that leaves home during times of drought; both long to return with the rains. It is sung here by Luiz's son, Gonzaguinho, who died tragically in 1991.

The disc moves to and fro between the rustic and cosmopolitan. Jackson do Pandeira created music based on regional rhythms like coco coupled with rapid-fire onomatopoeic singing and girlie choruses, a style heard here on **Tum-Tum-Tum**, with its blasts of brass punctuating both solos and chorus, and **Chiclete com Banana**. The latter was a huge 1970s hit for tropicália star Gilberto Gil and covered by merengue bands all over Latin America. Jorge de Altinho adds pumping bass lines to the rapid and upbeat **Bom Demais**, an accordion feast performed by Dominguinhos, another pretender to the Gonzaga throne, who reappears on **Querubim** and **Vou Com Você**.

A new generation of women singers came into their own on these songs. Composer Nando Cordel, who helped fuse forró into mainstream pop and merengue, performs **É de Dar Água na Boca** with the singer Amelinha. Most dramatic of all is the charismatic Elba Ramalho, who sings the sweet **Sanfonina Choradeira** with Gonzaga – a celebration of the irresistible music of their "brown lands".

Jan Fairley

Further listening: Sixteen groups and solo singers mix traditional and super-modernist versions of forró on **Baião de Viramundo – Tribute to Luiz Gonzaga** (Sterns). A wonderful variety of regional forró can be heard on **Brazil: Forró, Music For Maids and Taxi-drivers** (World Circuit)

96

Various Artists

Cuba I Am Time

Blue Jackal, 1999

Features the lexicon of leading twentieth-century Cuban musicians.

Few expensive box sets are worth recommending in a market flooded with compilations, but an exception has to be made for **Cuba I am Time**, a Cuban musical bonanza. Packaged, exquisitely, like a bright red cigar box, it contains four CDs and a beautifully illustrated, 111-page booklet – with a row of fat Cohibas on the cover – that documents not only the music and the musicians, but also the instruments and religious traditions. Every new musical craze is illuminated in text and pictures. It's a remarkable achievement.

Cuban Invocations, the first disc, introduces the African legacy in Cuban music through mystical songs dedicated to the *orishas* (deities), and also showcases Afro-Cuba's secular music, rumba, with its characteristic percussion and voice accompaniment. A favourite is Mercedita Valdés's hypnotic chant to **Obatala** (the *orisha* of peace and justice). On a grander scale are three leading modern folkloric troupes: Clave y Guaguancó with **La Voz de Congo**, Los Muñequitos de Matanzas with **Chacho**, and the sophisticated globe-trotters, Conjunto Folklórico Nacional de Cuba, with **Yemaya**. In semi-secular mode, the country singer Celina González praises her warrior god with **Que Vive Chango!**, while Los Van Van take santería into the nightclubs with an upbeat **Soy Todo**.

Cantar En Cuba (Cuban Song) covers nearly all the genres in Cuba's history, from those vehicles for news and political comment, canción and trova, to the archetypal son form, which expresses themes of love and desire – as well as dancing and politics. The disc opens with the pioneering 1930s singer-songwriter María Teresa Vera singing **Arrolla Cubano**. Joseíto Fernández performs the original **Guajira Guantanamera** while Cuarteto d'Aida, the 1950s girl group that launched Omara Portuondo, sing four-part harmonies on **Yo Si Tumbo Caña**. From the roots of son, Trío Matamoros perform the achingly nostalgic **Son de la Loma** in gentle harmonies of voice and guitar. The *septetos* Nacional and Habanera add two evergreens, now with a trumpet at the helm. Bringing son into the present, are the leading *soneros* (son singers), Adalberto Alvárez and Issac Delgado.

Bailar Con Cuba (Dance With Cuba) could hardly begin anywhere else than with **Qué Bueno Baila Usted** (How Well You Dance), legendary singer and dancer Beny Moré's catchiest mambo. Three sensational mambo and cha-cha-cha pioneers reveal their original brilliance: Orquesta Aragón's **Pare Cochero** is shamelessly romantic; Cachao underpins **Sociedad Antonio Maceo** and **Mulata Revoltosa** with his double bass; and Arsenio Rodríguez leads with his tres guitar on the earthy mambo, **Adivínalo**. Modern innovator Juan Formell leads Los Van Van to his songo beat on **Qué Sorpresa** while José Luis Cortés leads NG La Banda on **La Bruja Camara**, which parades the very newest timba craze.

Cubano Jazz, the last disc, charts Afro-Cuban jazz from its beginnings in the 1940s, with Mario Bauzá's high-energy **Mambo**. Post-Castro Afro-Cuban jazz inventor, Chucho Valdés illustrates his brilliance on Irakere's **Mil Ciento**. Following in his wake are Jesús Alémany and pianist Gonzalo Rubalcaba. The box closes on a futuristic collaboration between Brooklyn saxophonist Steve Coleman and master rumba drummers and singers, Afro-Cuba de Matanzas. A must-have luxury item.

Sue Steward

Further listening: La Bodeguita del Medio (Riverside Records) features music recorded in Havana's tiny old bohemian bar, including Revolutionary songs by Carlos Puebla.

97

Various Artists

Cumbia, Cumbia

World Circuit, 1989

Rodolfo y su Típica, Gabriel Romero, Armando Hernández y su Conjunto, Adolfo Echeverría y su Orquesta, Pedro Laza, Conjunto Típico Vallenato, Los Immortales, La Sonora Dinamita, Los Warahuaco, and others.

It is said that producer Nick Gold has the Midas touch, turning every album he approaches into golden mega-sellers. Nearly ten years before the historic *Buena Vista* sessions in Cuba, Gold's ear was focused on Colombia's most infectious dance rhythm, the cumbia. He poured through hundreds of recordings in the massive Discos Fuentes archive in Colombia and the resulting compilation, **Cumbia, Cumbia**, still stands as the finest of the genre.

The cumbia, Colombia's most famous musical style, is actually a term for a number of musical rhythms (including porro and puya) with their essence grounded in African percussion. The highly flirtatious dance associated with the style is thought to have begun in the festival of La Virgen de Canderia, held every February in Cartegena. It is traditionally a couple's dance: the men dress in white with a red handkerchief around their necks, while the women are dressed in long flowing skirts. The women also hold a candle and follow the men in a romantic pursuit, simultaneously fanning the flames by fanning their long skirts.

As recently as the first half of the twentieth century, the cumbia was considered vulgar and lower class – which was to say it came from the black coastal population – and the Colombian government shunned it for its foreign, especially Cuban, elements. It is ironic that in the years since, cumbia has gone on to become Colombia's national sound. This music, born of the coastal fishing villages, has gone on to incorporate waves of influences along the way, from the mambo-cumbias of the 1950s to today's hip-hop cumbia. It has also gone on to become one of the most popular genres in Latin America. A loping bass line combined with a driving brass section sets the tone for countless infectious Colombian numbers.

Cumbia, **Cumbia** features twelve classics from the 1950s through to the early 1980s. The album begins with Rodolfo's anthem, **La Colegiala**, a flirtatious song that, like so many of the best cumbias, is guaranteed to fill any dance floor. When the song was released, more than a quarter century ago, it swept Latin America, Spain and France, launching cumbia as one of the most popular global rhythms to emerge from South America.

The collection is a marvellous mix of veritable Colombian anthems such as Gabriel Romero's **La Piragua** and **La Subienda**, and Rodolfo's **Tabaco y Ron**, as well as passionate rootsy cumbias such as Pedro Laza's **Navidad Negra**. Here we see vintage Laza with a fishing tale straight from the Colombian coast – one of the most popular themes in cumbia – led by his percussion- and brass-driven orchestra, Los Pelayeros. Another gem is Armando Hernández's **Amaneciendo**, a song that brilliantly blends a salsa-tinged brass section and bouncy Latin jazz piano with Hernández's nasal voice.

In the years since the tracks on *Cumbia, Cumbia* were recorded, the trend in Colombia has drifted towards more electronic keyboards and drum machines. And while several of the tracks on this collection sound dated and tinny, the album remains a testament to a golden age of the genre, when infectious cumbia filled the airwaves and dance halls through all hours of the night.

Dan Rosenberg

Further listening: La Sonora Dinamita are Colombia's most quintessential and joyful cumbia big band – reach for **A Mover la Colita** (Riverboat Records) **Cumbias – Colombia's hip-swinging dance rhythm** (Rough Guides/World Music Network) features the broadest sweep of styles.

98

Various Artists

The Music of Puerto Rico: 1929–47

Harlequin/Interstate, 1992

Canario y su Grupo, Davilita, Los Jardineros, Los Reyes de la Plena, Sexteto Flores, Sexteto Okeh, Trio Borincano, and others.

In the first three decades of the twentieth century, New York's Upper East Side was transformed from a Jewish and Italian neighbourhood into a predominantly Puerto Rican community. A mass exodus of peasant farmers to New York had followed the US government's appropriation of land for sugar, leading to the growth of Spanish Harlem. Basement cellars became cigar-rollers' sweatshops and social clubs rang out with Spanish-style singing and guitar playing. Trios and small groups consoled audiences with lyrics about thatched huts and ox-carts; some criticised the state's actions. This compilation includes some of the earliest recordings of Puerto Rican music in the US.

The first musical focus was a grocery shop-cum-record store on 115th street, run by Victoria Hernández. In 1927, Victoria's brother Rafael arrived in town. An exceptionally talented composer, he wrote over two thousand songs, including the unofficial Puerto Rican national anthem, "Lamento Borincano" (Borinquen is the indigenous name for Puerto Rico). His first group, Trío Borincano, was modelled on popular Cuban son trios, with two harmonizing guitars and voices working to rhythms laid down by wooden claves. Borincano's first lead vocalist, Manuel "Canario" Jiménez, possessed a gloriously high falsetto tenor; after his departure, Hernández upgraded to a quartet, called Cuarteto Victoria, and hired Pedro Ortiz Davila, "Davilita", who appears here with

Conjunto La Plata on a quirky 1939 radio ad, **John Lahoud**.

Son was the most popular style in 1930s Spanish Harlem. Trios and quartets expanded into more powerful trumpet-led sextetos and conjuntos in imitation of Cuba. Sexteto Flores set to music a poem by Puerto Rican Lola Rodríguez, **Cuba y Puerto Rico**, sung here by Davilita: "Cuba and Puerto Rico are like a bird with two wings/They feel flowers and bullets in the same heart". Guitarist Pedro Flores embroiders the delicate melody on a traditional Puerto Rican cuatro guitar, a solo trumpet adds the Cuban touch and a marimbula (box bass) provides the surging rhythm.

In the mid 1930s, Canario broke the Cuban monopoly when he imported the plena – and launched a craze. These long, calypso-like narratives with their poetic, sometimes humorous lyrics brought him hit after hit. **Despiértese Manolao** – "wake up, Manolo, and milk your ox" – by Rafael Hernández, reveals Canario's vocal magic, his gorgeous warbling voice shadowed by Davilita's harmonies and Hawaiian-style choruses.

The plena was originally carried on jumpy accordion and guitar melodies, with maracas and claves threading bright cross rhythms. Los Reyes de la Plena maintained that line-up but added the pandero (frame drum) on **En La Ciento Dieciséis** (On 116th Street), a complaint about Prohibition. The inspiration for their mournful song **Caridad** (Charity) was the 1929 economic crisis. The singer's harsh tones and the guitarists' use of the bass strings create a sombre mood.

The album closes with one of several aguinaldos, Christmas carols, as sung on unfamiliarly freezing streets. The best-known, **Estrella de Oriente**, performed here by Sexteto Okeh, opens with a surreal sequence – a solo choral chant, the cry of the baby, the bleat of the animals at the crib, then joyful, upbeat dance music driven by an oom-pah brass band bass.

Sue Steward

Further listening: Canario y su Grupo's **Plenas** (Ansonia) reveals the catchy, topical plenas of 1930s Spanish Harlem. The Morales brothers' sublimely melodic **Los Tres Hermanos** (Ansonia) brought the sound of Puerto Rico's mountain hoe-downs into New York at around the same time.

99

Various Artists

Música Negra in the Americas

Network, 2000

Paracumbé, Ti-Coca, Andy Palacio, Vieja Trova Santiaguera, Luis Vargas, Lisandro Meza, The Jackson Singers, The Abyssinians, Mario Canonge, Duluc y Dominican, Issoco, Lugua & The Larubeya Drummers, Toto Bissainthe, The Congos, Septeto Raison, Erick Cosaque, Huracán de Fuego, and others.

A compilation that does its best to cover all of the genres represented in this book, and more, **Música Negra in the Americas** lists 33 tracks from 19 countries that form part of the African diaspora. This record topped the European World Music charts for two months in 2000. While a truly comprehensive look at "Black Music in the Americas" would probably take more like ten CDs, this two-disc set is a wonderful introduction to the region's musical richness, and full of top-notch studio recordings from commonly neglected regions.

The collection brilliantly combines Network's own previous productions with World Music icons such as Peru's Susana Baca (**Heces**), Brazil's Paulinho da Viola (**Coração Leviano**), and the Cuban Septeto Nacional (**Arrolla Cubano**), with equally talented but internationally overlooked artists such as Peru's Pepe Vásquez, Venezuela's Los Vasallos del Sol, and Guatemala's Jursino Cayetano.

Pepe Vásquez is the leading Peruvian singer and composer of his generation, and on **Ritmo de Negros** he mixes Afro-Peruvian folk forms such as lando and festejo with dynamic Afro-Caribbean salsa grooves – a trademark sound that has catapulted him to the top of Peru's music scene. The collection marked Jursino Cayetano's final recording session, made just before the Guatemalan guitarist's health began to fail. On **Buenas Noches Numadagu**, he exquisitely balances his delicate voice and subtle guitar technique with the deep and punchy Garifuna drums.

One of the most moving tracks is Grupo Vocal Desandann's percussion-backed a capella, **Guédé Nibo**. The group is part of the large Haitian minority in Cuba and sings primarily in Haitian creole with touches of Spanish. What they lack in instruments they more than make up for with their spectacular vocal skills, as they do in this haunting song for the Haitian Day of the Dead.

The collection also features notable recordings from legends such as Manny Oquendo y Libre (New York's leading Puerto Rican salsa-plena orchestra), Colombian diva Totó La Momposina, and the late Trinidadian calypso-singer, Growling Tiger. The latter's biting social commentary, **Money is King**, is a throwback to the 1930s, before electric guitars, drum-kits and keyboards began to dominate the calypso scene, and comes from a landmark session where he was joined by renowned Cuban trumpeter, Chocolate Armenteros, and Puerto Rican cuatro player, Yomo Toro.

Carmen González's **Caramba** shows that the legacy of slavery reached even Ecuador's Pacific coast. The percussion and mesmerizing Afro-marimbas come from the coastal city of Esmereldas, the centre of black culture in Ecuador. "Caramba" has become almost an anthem for singer Carmen González, perfectly matching her passionate voice with the percussive energy of the Esmereldan coast. The song is a challenge – she asks the marimbas and the drums to call out and demand "Caramba!" (Damn it!), calling for an end to poverty and indifference.

Música Negra In the Americas is a window into the diverse and wonderful musical styles of Latin America and the Caribbean.

Dan Rosenberg

Further listening: Africa in America (Discos Corasón) is a worthwhile three-disc set covering the roots of black music in the Americas, dominated by field recordings. Pepe Vásquez's **Ritmo de Negros** (Network) is a perfect sample of the contemporary Afro-Peruvian scene.

100

Various Artists

Paranda: Africa in Central America

Erato Detour, 2000

Paul Nabor, Junie Aranda, Jursino Cayetano, Gabaga Williams, Aurelio Martínez, Lugua Centeno, Dale Guzman, Andy Palacio, and others.

Paranda is a drumming rhythm with West African origins and also a style of music that dates back to the nineteenth century, when the Afro-Central American Garifuna people arrived in Honduras. It was there they first encountered Latin music and incorporated acoustic guitars, adding touches of Latin and Spanish rhythms to the music. Paranda reached its prominence in the early part of the twentieth century, and has changed little since, with its line up of large, wooden, barrel-shaped Garifuna drums, shakers, scrapers, turtle shell percussion and acoustic guitar.

Very few *paranderos* (players of paranda) are alive today, most of them old people aged sixty and above, living in rural areas far from recording studios. In Central America, like most parts of the world, the younger generation has fallen in love with Western pop, or derivatives like punta rock, which has vestiges of Garifuna influences. These sessions are essentially a Buena Vista Social Club of Garifuna paranda, and also the first trip into the recording studio for elderly guitarists Paul Nabor (73), Jursino Cayetano (61), and Junie Arranda (60). They were joined by punta vocalist Andy Palacio, guitarist Aurelio Martínez and master percussionist Lugua Centeno for a session that could be described as "Garifuna Unplugged", a sound combining African percussion, Cuban Son, American Blues, and West African guitar music all wrapped into one.

Paul Nabor is the last living *parandero* in Punta Gorda, and one of just six Garifuna in Central America who still perform. At 73, and in ill health, he still gets up every day at five in the morning, puts on his wide-brimmed straw hat, fetches his oars and heads out into the Caribbean to fish. He returns in the afternoon, when he can be found singing in front of a small thatched building, the Punta Gorda Garifuna Temple (Nabor in fact leads his congregation here on weekends). One of the most moving songs on the album is his **Naguya Nei**, a song that has become a virtual anthem in Punta Gorda. With a raspy yet passionate voice, he sings: "Dear brother, I am ill. I have tossed and turned in my bed. With this ailment, in the presence of my family, I have spoken to my children. Dear brother, when I pass away, they must have a band at my funeral to play this song…"

Paranda also features an impeccable performance from Guatemalan guitarist Jursino Cayetano. **Balandria** opens in trademark Garifuna style, with turtle-shell percussion, call-and-response vocals, clicks of glass bottles and the roar of the wide Garifuna drums before the tender and delicate voice of the ageing Cayetano kicks in with the galloping, bass-driven acoustic beat. Also noteable are the tracks featuring Lugua Centeno, famed in Central America as the greatest Garifuna drummer and the bandleader of the Larubeya Drummers. With songs such as **Fiura** he pays tribute to his late father's paranda compositions with his charismatic booming voice.

As the six paranda legends take their turn behind the mike, it becomes clear that these recording sessions were more than just historic, they were magical. Sadly, as several of the artists are now in ill health, it may well prove to be the only time they will ever record together.

Dan Rosenberg

Further listening: Lugua Centeno's band, Lugua and the Larubeya Drummers. hammer out fierce paranda rhythms on the intense **Bumari** (Stonetree) **Music from Guatemala Vol. 2: Garifuna** (Caprice) features a wide range of Garifuna music, from rootsy tracks to full-blown punta rock.